BEST GAY POETRY

2008

Best Gay Poetry

2008

edited by

Lawrence Schimel

A MIDSUMMER | LETHE
NIGHT'S PRESS | PRESS

New York, NY & Maple Shade, NJ

Pages 138-140 constitute an extension of this copyright page.

Published by Lethe Press in coedition with A Midsummer Night's Press.
All rights reserved. For information or permission to cite, contact:
Lethe Press, 118 Heritage Ave, Maple Shade NJ 08052
lethepressbooks.com   lethepress@aol.com

A Midsummer Night's Press, 16 West 36th Street, Second Floor
New York NY 10018
amidsummernightspress.com   amidsummernightspress@gmail.com

Printed in the U.S.
First printing, December 2008

Cover Photo by Massimo Caregnato
Cover Design by Diego Areso
Book design by Toby Johnson

ISBN 1-59021-128-6 / 978-1-59021-128-1

- -

Library of Congress Cataloging-in-Publication Data

Best gay poetry 2008 / edited by Lawrence Schimel.
      p. cm.
  ISBN-13: 978-1-59021-128-1 (alk. paper)
  ISBN-10: 1-59021-128-6 (alk. paper)
  1. Gay men--Poetry. 2. Gay men's writings, American. I. Schimel,
Lawrence.
  PS591.G38B47 2008
  811'.60803526642--dc21

                                    2008049784

TABLE OF CONTENTS

Introduction

Ten years ago, I began trying to interest a publisher in this anthology series, a project which I wanted first and foremost as a reader: something to collect all the myriad gay poems published in journals and collections I might not know about (or might not have seen, even knowing about them). A sort of one-stop-shopping (or in this case reading) experience, highlighting the best in gay poetry for each year.

Aside from the work which is published in gay periodicals or anthologies, and which is relatively easy for the gay reader to track down, there are many gay poets out there who are writing, and often publishing, work which is relevant and interesting as gay poetry, but which is often published in non-gay venues, making a project such as this anthology necessary, or at least useful: a sort of roadmap.

Publisher after publisher sent back the proposal, saying that while it looked like a prestige project there just wasn't enough of a viable market for poetry (and especially gay poetry). Over the years, I'd tinker with the proposal, updating references and marketing strategies, and send it off again; eventually it would be sent home again with yet another polite rejection, wishing me better luck with another house.

When I finally started my own one-man poetry press, A Midsummer Night's Press, I decided to put my money where my mouth is and publish the collection myself.

It is a project I still believe deeply in, despite the lack of interest from other publishers over the years.

And given the response from poets, it is something that many gay writers seem to embrace wholeheartedly. With luck, readers will also discover this anthology and find herein work which speaks to them. It is my hope that a collection such as this will appeal not just to those readers of poetry who already exist, but to the casual gay reader who might not be a fan of poetry, per se, but is willing to sample poetry that speaks to his experience in a relevant way. Likewise, that non-gay readers will turn to the volume for a (perhaps voyeuristic) glimpse of what concerns gay poets are writing away.

I am aware that a series like this takes a few years to establish itself, and I am willing to give the series time to do so, knowing that the earlier volumes will sell few copies while the series is getting its legs under itself and finding an audience.

And also building a name for itself within the writing community. A number of publishers of books or periodicals don't trust us yet, either as a press with so few published titles or as an anthology series which has not yet published its first volume (and which, due to various health and personal concerns, has unfortunately been much delayed, thereby seeming to confirm their mistrust). I hope that seeing the first book, these publishers submit their gay-interest titles for consideration (both for possible reprints as well as for the round-up section) for future volumes.

That said, this volume is not merely a precursor or draft to a later more-complete volume; I have tried to be as complete as I can be, although admittedly my reading of work that has not been submitted is not as wide as I might otherwise like (I have lived in Madrid, Spain for the past ten years, and my access to many English-language journals and periodicals—not to mention books—is thereby limited).

I do, however, see this anthology as being a part of a larger dialogue, both within the world of poetry as well as within the world of gay literature. As such, over the years, I expect the volumes to "speak" to one another in various ways, and am certain my own criteria will be influenced by the criticism and praise that each successive volume engenders.

I have tried to be broad in my selection criteria, striving for inclusiveness rather than to champion one particular school of poetics. (Admittedly, I am not a strong reader of prose poems, although there were very few submitted this year.) Despite the singular noun in the title, I hope for this series to highlight the best of gay poetries, in all its poetic diversity as well as with regard to the gay subjects and themes addressed.

Given the broad array of subjects, themes, and forms, there is no easy way to order such a collection; the book is arranged alphabetically by author's surname, which will hopefully result in readers finding unexpected surprises both in the juxtapositions between poems and in the act of reading either systematically through from beginning to end or skipping around to first read poems by familiar names (or unfamiliar ones, depending on individual taste).

I would like to take a moment to thank all the poets

who submitted work for this project, for sharing the faith in this project, and to invite them and others to continue to submit any relevant gay poetry for each year's new collection. I would also invite readers of poetry to bring to my attention poems they think I should be considering.

I would also like to thank Steve Berman of Lethe Press, who stepped in to help with co-publishing this volume when other concerns prevented me from continuing with the project solo. And to Toby Johnson for his heroic efforts on the production side, and to Diego Areso for the cover design.

And finally, a thanks to you, the reader, for your interest in gay poetry and this anthology.

—Lawrence Schimel
Madrid, Spain
November 2008

Best Gay Poetry

2008

Antler

In Front of Everyone

Tired, O tired of "cocksucker"
    having a negative connotation,
Of persons demeaned and degraded
    by being called cocksucker,
As if it was something awful to be,
    something you should be
        ashamed of,
    loathsome, repugnant, sleazy,
When it turns out it's the reverse,
    exactly the opposite.
Speak the word cocksucker clearly,
    proudly, sweetly, kindly, warmly
        the way a child says
    Mommy, Daddy, Jesus.
Let the word cocksucker replace the word God
    for 2000 years to make up for 2000 years
        Christianity believed
    cocksucking a sin,.
Let the word cocksucker replace the word America
    to make up for all the years
        cocksucking was a crime in America.
Let the word cocksucker replace the word soldier
    to make up for all the cocksuckers
        killed by soldiers
    screaming "cocksucker!"
Let the word cocksucker replace the word sucker
    so that instead of a mother telling her son
        "I'll give you a sucker if you're good"

14

a mother telling her boy
            "I'll give you a cocksucker if you're good."
Bring babies to see a boy's cock being sucked off.
Bring old men and women in wheelchairs to see
            a boy's cock being sucked off.
Bring the just-dead into a room
            where passionate 69 is taking place
                        because hearing is the last sense to go
            and you want to honor the just-dead
with the slurping sounds of cute boys
            who are serious about each other.
Let a boy's cock being sucked off be the minister
            who conducts the wedding service
                        and asks the questions
            of the two young men
                        to which they reply "I do"
            and then kiss each other
in front of everyone.

Rane Arroyo

Slow Change

I thought, it's done, I'm out.
My father died, the women in
my life married, my bed got
busy, and I wore no scarlet G.
Waitresses hit on me, sorry
I'm. Employers googled me,
so you're. I hired a skywriter,
yes I'm. I took out ads, I'm.

*

Sometimes I remember the closet:
that spiritual corset, that cruel jock,
telephone/confessional booth, coffin
for dark rehearsals, tomb without
a name, bomb shelter inside my mind.
Sometimes I forget the closet and
step outside into the world. Men look
at me, *are you?* Yes, I'm not an idea.

John Barton

Fences

Paul Cadmus (1904-1999),
egg tempera on pressed wood panel, 1946

What holds men apart is seldom just

    Sleep, afternoons at Saltaire not often as
      Tranquil, warm salty air still as water in a glass

Barely a soul to come between, you the one
    Sprawled half awake under a blanket on sand
      Powdery as ground embers of sugar, the other drowsy

Leaning from a fencepost as if
    Lashed—poised, he daydreams, for arrows

     Of heat to pierce his side ardently

Flesh thirsting after sacrifices anyone he knows well
    Too quickly sates, desire thinning headlong into the
          cloudless

    Sun, clothes at his feet dropped from the rampant
Form his body unshyly attenuates, torso
    Flared upwards from the waist around the voracious

    Lungs of a jaguar, skin a sail
Snapping fast about his ribs, nipples carried high

   On the chest's expansive surf, reverie pitching

    Chin forwards, hands clasped behind
Post and back, wrists unbound yet the mind in

Frustration cinches them tight, the overhead
    Hypnotic roar of the tide
Crashing ashore, vestiges of bark above his head skinned

    Away by half-imaginary breezes, knots
        In the post so sun-stroked and smooth they glow

Broken fencing uncoiling away in directionless

    Waves across the dunes, thin slats unable to
        Hold back heat, its scorching

Onslaught relentless, though sand is still
    Yet to rise stinging, freshets
        Of air exhaled from the sea, the erosion of all

He might desire unbuoyed by tumbled
    Echoes bounced down the barbwired stuporous

    Miles of beach while you slumber speechless

Between slatted lines of every drifting thought
    Any narrow stretch of sand where you could wake

    Abandoned between weather-beaten verticals
Lopsided and in want of redress, so very
    Little of this landscape left unravished inside the long
        familiar

    Wind-shined climes of your flesh.

Dan Bellm

The Crossing
(Exodus 13: 17-18)
for Congregation Sha'ar Zahav, San Francisco

God did not lead us by the nearer way
when Pharaoh let the people go at last,
but roundabout, by way of the wilderness—

pillars of fire and cloud marking night and day—
to the edge of the flood tide—uncrossable and vast.
If God had led us by the nearer way,

we cried, *we wouldn't die here; let Egypt oppress
us as it will; let us return to the past.*
But we have come out, by way of the wilderness,

in fear; on faith; free now, because we say
we are free; no longer the unchosen, the outcast.
God did not lead us by the nearer way,

but into rising waters, which do not part unless,
with an outstretched arm, we step forward, and stand fast.
Roundabout, by way of the wilderness,

we have come, blessed with love, lesbian, gay,
or sanctified in ways of our own, to bless
our God, who did not lead us by the nearer way,
but roundabout, by way of the wilderness.

David Bergman

The Embrace

To hold you is not
to contain you much
less possess you it
is a way to be
in contact with that
part of you that is
body and sense by
addition that part
of you that is not
how even your breath
bears traces of life
that is more than air
more than this heat more
than the rasp of words
I imagine I
can hear which may not
be words at all but
merely your presence
drawn across the flesh
the self abraded
by what else it is
and must always be

Jericho Brown

Because My Name Is Jericho

You would not believe me if I told you
       I met a man called Joshua.

I am not a city nor a saint.
       He knew where my body had been.

I named each place. Then after a long silence
       He played a song for me on his trumpet.

       There is a word

     You will not have me say. So my mouth plays
Now as it did then, open,

     The broken bell of a tossed horn—
Each eye, my entire body, struck

     Open, dry
As it was that night. And maybe you're

     Right. Something had to be taken
From me. I was too beautiful

     To be such a sinner. He must have hated me
For that. Maybe some of us are

     Better broken into—we mend
Easy as a ripped shirt or

     A damaged wall.
If ever asked about damage I will tell

     What I tell myself. I am overwhelming.
He was overwhelmed.

      See. I am just as much a man
As Joshua. I've got the silence to prove it.

James Cihlar

The Estate Auction

You asked me to go with you
to an estate auction thirty miles south.
I still can't get over your car:
late sixties Impala, rust-free,
big as a barge. You told me
about riding with your twin,
how you would lay your head
in his lap as he drove.
After I moved in, he would call
and leave messages like,
"Watch *Night Court,* it's funny."
We stopped at a Dairy Queen
on the way, probably the same one
I stopped at ten years later
with a student, on our way to a reading,
thinking how far away I'd gotten
from myself. Then we drove
through a town called Friend,
with the sign, You've Got a Friend
in Friend. The auction was a bust,
tables of orange sunburst jewelry
and green pressed glass.
It was a chance to hold hands
in the car, I guess,
listen to the radio play "Precious and Few,"
like we did the night I told you
why I did not want to move in,
or like we did at the theater,

watching *Murphy's Romance,*
my jacket thrown over our hands.

Jeffery Conway

The Play

When the boy playing the goat
had his artificial penis jerked-off
by the boy playing the young virgin
gypsy girl, and the faux "semen"
shot in our direction from the dimly-lit
stage, I began to worry if I'd made
the right theatrical choice for our
evening out. I shook in my seat
from beginning to end (stifled
laughter), but you, sophisticate,
Hollywood power lawyer, forced
courtesy-laughs, checked your watch.
I'd hoped the pricey surf 'n' turf
at the intimate West End café
would redeem me in your greenish eyes.
Later, at your rented cottage, I built
a fire that wouldn't catch. We drove
from one closing convenience store to
another: no Duraflame logs available,
apparently, in August, at seaside resorts.
"Doesn't matter," you confessed
as we pulled into the driveway,
"I can't do this anyway." Your cell phone
rang—your boyfriend from the other coast.
"I'll wait," I said, and climbed the narrow steps
to the rooftop deck: foghorn, cool breeze,
full moon in Capricorn, all of these
kept me company until you reappeared,
apologetic, and kissed me into a frenzy.

"I can't," you said, pulling away, "if we
do this again, it'll be something more."
I looked toward the beam-lit sea.
"Is it ever 'something more'? I should go."
As I descended the stairs, I heard you call out
"No, don't." I walked home
trying to avoid eyes of men who cruised
under street lights made unimportant
by the glow of the counterfeit spotlight
coming down from way above.

Steven Cordova

Across a Table

"I'm glad you're positive."
"I'm glad you're positive,

too, though, of course, I wish
you weren't." I wish you weren't

either is the response I expect,
and you say nothing.

And who can blame you?
Not me. I'm not the one

who'll call you after dinner and a movie.
You're not the one who'll call me.

We both know we have
that–what?–that ultimate date

one night to come, one bright morning.
Who can blame us? Not the forks

and not the knives that carry on
and do the heavy lifting now.

Jeff Crandall

Hybrid

A bird and a fish may fall in love, but where
will they build their house? — Proverb

Say I'm a penguin, and he is a flying fish.
Certainly there is some overlap?

Given the planet's biodiversity
more likely I am an emu
and he is a swordfish, some lone pelagic wanderer.
But this excludes the possibility
of even the remotest encounter.
So let us consider the joints and seams of the world,
where air presses down on water and water
kisses back, say, a pond.

Then he is a catfish prowling the shoreline
beneath the water's palpable membrane
black body all whisper, mystery and feeler.
And I am a mallard, oblivious paddler
skimming the surface of its lovely, edible scum.

When our eyes meet
through the silver film of that mirror,
the inevitable, unstoppable synaptic pulse
electrifies as the slick, undulant muscle of his body
curves like a tongue along my belly.

And who needs a weave of marshgrass,
a nest of pebbles to contain this
irrational, impossible, heady bliss?

James Crews

How to Write a Love Poem

You must step outside the night, look in
and become the harmless, lonesome voyeur
standing in your own backyard. Watch

the two figures move inside and listen
to their familiar voices straining with music
through the screens. Always live between

the moment the lover places the needle
on Billie Holiday's "Fine and Mellow," then
takes your hand, and the moment his sleep

spreads its dark throughout the apartment,
everywhere but the quiet corner in which
you write by flashlight. And because of this

betweenness, windows will open themselves
constantly in your poems. Men will look out
and look in like the man now standing

in the damp grass below this window.
Do not notice him as he fills his notepad
describing how these two figures silhouette

themselves against orange lamplight, moving
in time to *Love will make you and make you.*
He records laughter and the precise arc as one

body dips another; he writes down cricket-drone,
streetlight and the scurrying of cockroaches
back into cracks in the pavement as he steps

closer, and the lover pulls the shade, then
takes both of you, at once, into his arms.

Brian Cronwall

Barebacking

Some evening or afternoon or night,
in a maze room or candlelit bedroom,
some moment of tongue
on five-o'clock-shadow and sweat
or clutches of purple moans and smiles,
you'll probably do it: in spite of what you know,
have read, heard, told the educator or your therapist,
though you have a Trojan under the key band
or in the laquered box on the nightstand,
despite your pledges of "risk management"
and "harm reduction," you'll do it.
He'll be amazing, or look negative, so
you'll just what-the-hell with him anyway,
it's just one time; his touch is fire and lava,
juicing peach and salty beer, tobacco
breath after decades of only dreaming of smoking,
sea-mist as smooth as moss, your and his fingers
traveling continent to island to sea,
caught in kelp-beds wrapped around limbs,
his dark focused eyes and yours wetly watching:
you will forget to remember and remember to forget
alternatives as you slowly ripen into each other's
pistils and stamens, buzzing crescendo swarms,
closer then closer to that eager moment when
you will yes-by-god do it, the moment before
the worrying will begin all over again.

Steve Fellner

I Am Known As Walt Whitman

To the gay men who spend their Friday nights lurking in
                    the cyber chatroom, I am known
as Walt Whitman. My alias. My secret identity. My
                    better half.
Somewhere in that claim a stupid joke can be found.
                    Don't expect me

to discover it. I'm too busy on-line looking for the man
                    who offered my boyfriend
his first taste of crystal meth. It got him so messed up he
                    couldn't stop
meeting men off the internet, and then begging them to
                    stay after they had their release.

Of course, they always left. Bored, he did other risky
                    things
like having sex in a bathroom stall at Wal-Mart where he
                    was arrested
for indecent exposure. (Somewhere on those tiles there is
                    a trace of him.)

He lost his job as a minimum wage earning bagboy at
                    Wegman's, causing him
to avoid the grocery story altogether, the only one in
                    town. Crystal kidnaps
your hunger anyway. His appetite resurfaced elsewhere.

Like in orgies where condoms were thought of as
                    unnecessary ornaments.

(Somewhere in my voice, useless empathy can be found.)
He contracted HIV.
I broke up with him because I didn't want to take care of
someone who was going to die

in such an uninspired way. Somewhere in this narrative
there may be a shred of logic to be found. O, my dumb
dead boyfriend,
you are my expired muse. Because I know you gave so
kindly to strangers, I imagine

your hole as raw as the material for this poem. Bloody
and needy and lovely.
Somewhere in your flesh I had wished to find a reason to
forgive you. Somewhere
in your grave I will find the redemption I'll need for
hating you.

Somewhere in another poem I will find the strength to
tell this story
without invoking the name of Walt Whitman. But now I
need him. I need that dead
homosexual to find a way into my prayer for you. I can't
let this be a poem about me

and you. It needs to be something larger. Something that
moves our words
beyond a story of drugs, a memoir of lonely people, a
poem of catharsis.
Are you listening from the heavens, my worthless love:

Walt Whitman wrote those poems about desire and flesh
and never felt any better.

Somewhere in that knowledge a lesson can be found. But
                          now
all we have are these words, words which will not be
                     remembered

by any more than a few hungry readers, words which will
                       disappear
as quickly as the instant message in a chatroom, words
                     that will be as unrecognizable
as the misunderstood ones in what was once someone's
                  meaningless, necessary poem.

John Frazier

Once

I've never seen someone shit, I say to my boyfriend as he begins
to close the bathroom door with his right index finger, already lowering

himself on the toilet. I want to be asked to witness the white briefs
bunch at his ankles, the hairy legs spread, his face turn in a grimace.

But you've lived with men, he replies. I don't want
to be vulgar, I say, eyeing his balls, waiting

for an invitation. Even as I defend my ignorance—how I grew up
in a house of prudish women, how the impossible boys I dated

never showed me this—I know it's not true. I saw my father squat once
over the porcelain toilet in the old house the summer it burned,

the muscles in his thighs tensing. Why does everything
come back to this man, I think, even at this age?

And now hours later while doing the dishes I've been thinking
this is what I will do, love the worst parts of the men who
                              come home to me.

Brad Gooch

Moon River

We get along best when we're both asleep
Back to back, head to head, knee to elbow,
The etiquette is light, the choreography deep,
We've gone where men before us feared to go.
Down into the cave where Orpheus descended,
Hand in hand, not solitary, but very slow.
Hell's different with a partner, not so bent.
The writing on the wall has an enchanted, fiery glow,
Like the neon logo of a trendy new restaurant
Written up in the *New York Times* or *Zagat*,
Domesticated by something as simple as a pair of pants
XL, legs long, and on your head, my ski hat.
In the middle of the night I whispered your name.
Or was it my own? They feel about the same.

Jeremy Halinen

My City

after Tony Hoagland

When I think of what I know about Spokane,
I think of beating my boyfriend's best friend
in the Safeway parking lot one evening,

between a Honda Accord and a cart return.
One moment making car talk, the next
my fist curving up to meet her

unsuspecting, smiling face. It was a sort of
  violent
surprise
that a bloody nose could turn me on

so much I'd wish I were straight enough
to take her home. Behind her
I could see the moon

rising slowly above Maple Street,
and I thought of my boyfriend, who always tries
to be good in every situation,

that such noble effort ought to be emulated.
Then I slammed my fist against her frown,
against all the time he'd thrown away on her.

My knuckles reveled in that moment, in the wetness

I'd always known she hid within.
When she fell to the asphalt below me

and tried to crawl away, begging
mercy, I bent and slapped her neck
until she asked me why. Then I wiped

my hands on her long brown hair
and went inside to shop. And who was left
to give her answer? And who would know

what, or how, to say?

James Allen Hall

Wake

I called my grandfather "Pa," back when he'd pull me
atop his bony shoulders, then charge across my childhood
yard, fall in a pile of leaves where we'd roll, laughing,
his hands tickling me until I could not breathe.

The last time we spoke, we yelled obscenities over local
phone lines. He'd been arrested for soliciting sex
from young boys in a public park. My boyfriend and I disguised
our voices, called him the first night out of jail, saying
"You're paying for this pizza, asshole, or we'll kill you."

No one cried at the wake except for one woman, an ex-lover,
and she cried hard, outlasting even the hymns. Afterwards,
my uncle drove the hearse back, clicking on the radio.

Back home, the aunts were setting out too much food
on picnic tables, and boy cousins chased girl cousins
through thick stalks of corn. I walked my mother away
from the grave. And when, at the car, we could still hear
the ex-mistress sobbing to High Heaven, my mother stopped still.
She'd been serene through the service.

I knew enough by then to understand my family
were a ruthless, dramatic people; I knew I couldn't stop her.
Her heels left spiked stars in the hard earth,
marching back to the unburied coffin, yelling,

Do you know where he put his cock?, leaning down to
                              strike her enemy.

At the last moment she quieted, she steadied her hand,
straightening her black dress. But the woman turned,
and my mother slapped her. Twice, saying, In me. In me,
                              as hard as she could.

Then, because the silence she'd created was the silence
                              she'd lived
so buried beneath, my mother heaved the fancy vases
straight down into the exposed plot, she wasn't satisfied
until glass vomited out the open mouth.

Forrest Hamer

Blue

And then comes longing,
a man you've known
but have not really met,

who whispered Portuguese
minutes after making love,
folding around you like skin.

The longing comes and
never arrives, imagines you
and never is revealed;

it shapes your body
into someone lonely, rains
upon your house like August.

Reginald Harris

Trailer Park Self-Portrait
(Mobile, Alabama, 1983)

Hmmm...I bet you're really
Straight...You're all man he
whispers in the dark *I bet*
you don't get fucked he whispers
unbuttoning, unzipping *I bet*
you have a big dick he
whispers, reaching *You like*
to fuck all night he whispers,
salivating *I bet I'd like*
to take it all night too...I
sure would like to try

I cannot see myself in his blue eyes

In the dark he whispers *Sorry*
but you have to go My
family you know he whispers
buttoning, zipping *They*
know, you know he whispers,
reaching *how I'm...guys...you*
know they're cool...but this...
he whispers wiping up *but you...*
a black man...you in the dark
he whispers *you*
they wouldn't understand
Hmm... I don't even want to try

I cannot see myself in his blue eyes

Sean Horlor

In Praise of Beauty
—after Karen Solie

What we see shapes our imagining.

Poetry, clothes, a pop star's swagger.
    Cologne in glass bottles.

A man with eyes the colour
    Of a Eucalyptus leaf turned over.

A spotlight's preference
    For shimmer over shine.

For every act of daring
    The astonished eye chooses to praise.

And for all that drifts: shipwrecks,
    Lightning, a stranger's hello–

Beauty with edge.
    Beauty with consequence.

A kind of grief that separates our lives
    Into all that matters, then all that does not

And all it asks of you
    Is to look, to look twice, to keep looking.

Desire is lonely work.

Richard Johns

Missed Connections

1

Because of the snow
we were walking
on the street:
me one way,
you the other.
We suddenly
passed, and only
our glances met
when together we
turned to look
back. Years later
now when we cross
paths do you, like
me, still wonder
and regret? Is it
possible to meet?

2

Hurtling along in the
Underground, I was
holding on for life
in the swaying throng
when I spotted your
reflection. What was

it—shared
desire?—that made
you smile like that
and me smile back?
I should have stayed
to find out, but
my stop came. And
then you were pulling
away, and I couldn't
keep pace with
the train. Remember?

3

I was the one
with salt-and-
pepper hair
wrapt up in a
book at a table
near the window
who happened to
look up
when whoever you
were with—a
friend, perhaps, or
lover—stood up
and left for a
moment and you
glanced at me. In
that brief space
it was as if
we said things

with our eyes, like:
"Are you the
one?" Then: "Where do
we go from here?"
Which is why
I'm left wondering
now: Shouldn't we try
to find out? —You
know who you are.

4

I had followed you
into that room
of darkness and bodies
then—struggling
to move to
reach you: the
place made near
impassable with lust—I
lost you briefly
there. Men
everywhere—
putting their bodies on
again with
unbridled feeling,
inhabiting
the moment again
and again. Then
you were there: a
torso and crotch
being mouthed

in the darkness. Moving
in, I worked
your nipples hard
until you groaned
and knelt, unzipping
me to swallow
everything
I gave. Nothing
was missed. Only,
as soon as the moment
vanished so did
you. And yet,
nothing was missed, really,
nothing was missed.

Jee Leong Koh

Glass Orgasm

Dishwasher safe, the glass medical grade,
the dildo is hand-blown
from the same element as brandy balloons,
milk bottles, picture tubes and silicone
implants; in other words, it's made
of prose. The form is poetry.
It jabs as hard as Japanese harpoons
or, callipygian glide,
curves like the spine of the sperm whale,
so slick and sleek a slide.
The fired figure's ribbed with filigree:
a tree trunk ivied by plump veins,
a caterpillar's burrs,
carelessly rocky road or studded Braille,
or else it's scored by ruts and flutes.
(For Puritans, the glass also comes plain;
for Quakers, terse.)
More than mouth-pleasure, the lacunae gawk
at lattachino work, the twists
of lemon, gold and blue
inside, not painted on, the shoot
of fiberglass; the mists
compressed to chalk;
or the dichroic head unveiling two
blushes when viewed from different spots,
G or prostate.
Van Gogh's *The Starry Night* may wet one's thighs
but it's too rectangular and pastethick for a shot,
unlike the borosilicate.

Stars and moon etched on its glass eye,
it probes the ocean, a mammalian fish,
foraging for supernovas.
When it finds and swallows one—O, sweet jehovah
of light and heat and life and death and wish!
It passes—the light dims—out of the ass—
the heat cools—and so decompose,
though shatterproof, though in demand,
to soda, lime and sand,
the poetry and prose,
cut glass.

Timothy Liu

Consequential

Sitting down to a bottle we could
afford, I asked what would be worse:
if he died first, or I? Wouldn't it

be best if we just went together—
hijacked plane, avalanche? He
thought on this and replied: better

that you go first. This was the start
of a midlife crisis, not knowing
if we were at the middle or closer

to the end, our looks, our chances
of securing a love that's equal
to what we think we're able to give.

Chip Livingston

Let's Do This Again

We shared waking up; one of us had to be first
to open a sleepy eye, and spy on the other, proving
he was there, then to close it, denying thirst,
the urge to rise and pee, a day beginning after loving
lasted a whole night. Flesh found again
through wadded sheets – legs again, arms again.
Skin to skin again. Mouths again.
This could be routine if we don't panic,
follow urge to flee and ruin it,
take a different job and move away,
or find another lover somewhere along the way.
I'll keep this morning like a photograph –
you shaving at the sink, me watching from the bath.

Raymond Luczak

Instructions To Hearing Persons Desiring A Deaf Man

His eyebrows cast shadows everywhere.
You are a difficult language to speak.
His long beard is thick with distrust.
You are another curiosity seeker.
His hands are not cheap trinkets.
Entire lives have been wasted on you.
His face is an inscrutable promise.
You are nothing but paper and ink.
His body is more than a secret language.
Tourists are rarely fluent in it.
His eyes will flicker with a bright fire
when you purge your passport of sound.
Let your hands be your new passport,
for he will then stamp it with approval.
A deaf man is always a foreign country.
He remains forever a language to learn.

Ed Madden

Viscous

You find it after summer rains, amoebic sores
of yellow and orange on rolled bales of hay,
slime molds climbing the mounds of dead pasture.

Being a boy, being eight or ten, you call it
monkey vomit. Being a boy, and older than him,
you dare your brother to touch the stuff: touch it.

It doesn't quiver; you think it should. It glistens
and spreads, it waits. It palms the hay, caresses
the moist rot. Why are you afraid?

It will dry to a crust, fade to stain, disintegrate
in a dust of dry spore, like the semen
on your lover's body, viscous, glistening, briefly

alive—is it 1988? and if he were positive?
It's 1998. He is not your brother. You touch
the crust on slope of belly, thin crust like sugar,

taste like salt. Scrape it off, wonder is it yours, or his.

Jeff Mann

Relic

Not golden, not bejeweled, nothing like the reliquaries
of Munich's Residenz, Vienna's Hofburg,
those ornate receptacles for the flotsam and jetsam of
saints.
Only a cardboard box in the storage room
of my father's house in Hinton, West Virginia.
Inside, amidst occult tomes, rests what I retain
of you. The scrawled, seductive letters you sent
after moving with your husband to Massachusetts.
A thin album of photos, a few bottles of German wine we emptied.
The leather teddy bear you bought me in State College,
the silver pentagram ring you mailed me from Framingham,
a few flirtatious valentines. And—most intimate keepsake—
the last thing I asked from you, mere weeks before we parted—
a pair of your white jockey shorts.

What did I expect? That something precious could be saved?
Your taste, your scent? The mourning dove's dirge?
The way I felt, those larcenous afternoons?
The first pair of underwear you gave me,
cloth still moist from the gym, I slipped inside
a Glad bag, hoping to preserve your sweat.
Fanatic's error. The crotch-musk soon turned to folly,
the faint smell of mildew. Sheepish, I asked again.
The second pair? FTL's, tattered a bit. Folded neatly still
inside a box there is no reason to open any longer..

These briefs are scentless after fifteen years,

evidence not of beauty but of failure.
Something for my survivors to throw out
after I am over, souvenir meaningless to all
but me. I would like to lie here, say that once,
when I had you naked and bound, the way I loved you most,
I gagged you with this very garment, your own sweaty shorts,
then wrapped my arms about your hairy chest and,
as I entered you, relished your muffled moans, but
no, that never happened, that was only another ecstasy
our hurried time together did not allow,
one of many revelations we never got to share.
You gave me a pair of white jockey shorts,
you gave me what was easy to give,
reserving the rest for another. What I have left of you

is cotton white, stained by none of rapture's sap.
No longer a fabric I press to my face, no longer
a history of musk to breathe deep.
Flesh will never revisit the saints' finger bones.
Scent and warmth will return to this garment
no more than youth will, youth shared for six months,
then squandered apart. White as the heron
picking low tide for scraps, white as the skin
of buttocks beneath their fine coating of fur.
White, the waves' unscrolling epitaph.
White, the paper remaining when words run out.

Jaime Manrique

The Blue Hour

Sometimes here in Manhattan
in the early evening
as a helicopter or a seagull
slices the sky—I remember
my grandparents' town
when the hour
was an invitation
to the bats to enter our house
like a dark invasion
of tiny spaceships.

A blue light caresses
the brick wall
across from my window
and I get up from the bed
where you and I lie
and touch January's
frost on the glass.
You ask me
for the time, as if I—
like my grandfather—
could read the heavens.

It 's the blue hour
in Manhattan; we are in love
and I want the light
to trap us
like bees in amber.

Snow falling, I walk
with you to the avenue
helping you carry your luggage.
As we wait for a taxi
your eyes avoid mine—
you are returning
to your city of bridges and warm stars.

You climb into the cab.
As I watch you disappear,
You do not turn around—
as a final punctuation mark.
Later, at the corner nearest my house
I trip and almost crash
against the sidewalk. My shoulders
could prop up a brownstone.
They carry the full weight
of my fifty years.

Pablo Miguel Martinez

At the Pentecostal Baths

Tactile, yes. In total darkness, yes.
As if eclipsed. As on his lips.
As if in secret retreat,
finding his way, eagerly. Yes.

A room filled with men, yes.
Lightness years away.
He waits for the coming
of the Paraclete,

a proper businessman, yes,
on his knees, imploring,
waits for ecstasy, yes.
Glory revealed in silver-

dollar holes. Halos, yes.
Come with thy grace
and heavenly aid,
he begs.

There are no tongues
of flame. Is this
how it ends? This is
how it ends, yes.

John McCullough

The Bulldog Years

Slicing lemons, I feel the sting
of juice on a cut as Will moans about

his boyfriend moving out. Small wonder:
he never stops talking, hangs around here

to ogle boot boys, daddies,
lewd come-ons whispered

as they pass. I'm more worried
about myself. Why can't I stop listening

to Weird Will, lost souls and every other
nut who makes more noise than sense?

The Rhino's honking laugh explodes
and I yield again to drag queens

high on tequila, self-pity; bored rent boys
and Sandra whose girlfriend got addicted

to steroids, *roared off in her HGV to Greece.*
Their voices gush like wine taps

I can't turn off. *Yes, mate,* I say
as if they were my friends

though in a way they are: old sweethearts
whose quirks I've grown to love

too much. This foot of teak
doesn't separate but fuses us,

an unbreakable hinge. *Oi, you lot,*
the taxi driver yells, *anyone seen Ahmed?*

I shrug, mouth *Sorry* and turn
my ear again to Will's problem,

wipe the counter so thoroughly
I might be disinfecting a wound.

Billy Merrell

My Boyfriend Refuses to Speak in Iambic Pentameter

CHARACTERS

JEROME
JEFF
MOM
DAD
JEFF'S MOTHER
JEFF'S STEPFATHER

ACT 1

(The curtain's lifted, revealing a white room. It's empty and its walls are blank. Some music begins faintly in the background.

JEROME enters, carrying a box. He puts a poster on the wall. It's bright and colorful. He hangs some photographs. Another poster. A shelf. As he continues his work, the lights fade. A scrim is lowered between him and the audience. The music continues.)

*(SCENE: After a moment the scrim
is lifted and the lights rise, revealing
JEROME alone in his room. It no
longer looks like a set. It is a room.*

*JEROME sits on the floor,
photographs and magazines laid out
around him. He cuts images out of
each and collages them onto an old
guitar. He works slowly. The music
fades into the background.)*

I know it's real, but realize it's not you
who's here to help me see how well it works
without much ~~pain~~
               work, the way it follows through
without requiring that I follow ~~you~~.
                             Look,
at first it felt like we were tied together,
so if you walked out angry, I did too.
You stormed around; I learned to ~~watch the weather~~
                       notice whether
you ~~needed~~ me to cure or comfort you.
    wanted
I thought you thought that love would be a chore
the way you roll your eyes at photos of us,
but now I see you've always wanted more
than what your parents ~~have~~
                   had.

(JEROME *pastes the last of the images onto the guitar, then stands to look at it from farther away.*)

And you won't notice,
but there is one for every day we've shared.

(*He begins to clean up.*)
It seems my heart has always been prepared.

(*The lights fade to black.*)

(SCENE*: Out of the darkness, a faint blue light rises, revealing two boys' faces. They are sitting on the bed next to each other, close enough to be holding hands. They're watching a movie. The light flickers brighter revealing the two, each looking up at the clock occasionally, discreetly, so the other doesn't notice.* JEROME *smiles when* JEFF *catches him. He opens a window and a single firefly enters.*)

It seems my heart has always been prepared
for someone to sneak in, despite bad luck.
We each had closed our mouths, been truth-then-dared:
the next thing that we knew our mouths weren't shut.
And neither were our minds—

(*One, then another firefly blinks in through the open window. As the*

*boys sit there, several more crowd
in. When the clock finally strikes
midnight, there are countless fireflies
above their heads.* JEROME *pauses
the movie.)*

I'd always known...
And now I have to wonder how much time
I would have spent denying it, alone,
if you weren't there to put your mouth to mine.

(JEROME tells JEFF *to close his
eyes and reaches silently under the
bed. The fireflies surround them.)*

Sometimes I laugh, remembering your face
when I first pulled my lips away and smiled.
You gave yourself away, gave me a place
to put myself—at least for some short while.
And nearly one year later, here we are:
your eyes still closed, me holding your guitar.

(JEROME tells JEFF *he can open
his eyes. The lights fade, except for
the fireflies, which hover faithfully.
When the lights rise,* JEFF *is the one
holding the guitar.* JEROME *stands
facing him, holding a card that
reads "You Make Me Happier Than
Words Can Say.")*

My eyes are closed. You're holding your guitar.
(I've never felt so stupid in my life.)

I spent forever; you bought me a card
and wrote in it *You're great! Yours truly, Jeff.*
The thing is, I don't care how much you spent,
but all you did is pick it from a shelf
while I spent nights recalling how it went:
~~our kiss, our year.~~
You didn't even make the thing yourself.
How lame am I for thinking that you'd care,
for thinking this all means as much to you
when clearly you don't love me—or are you scared
to show me how you feel, to feel it too?
But as I go to say it, my eyes open.
I'm never sure when mine's the heart that's broken.

> (JEFF *sets the guitar on the bed and
> turns away.* JEROME *reaches for
> him and* JEFF *hides his face, then
> wipes his eyes and thanks him.)*

My heart, it seems, is not the heart that's broken.
To see his face, to see him standing there,
all guilt and puppy frown. I tell him *Look,
it's no big deal.* But he's beyond repair.

> (A firefly leaves through the
> window.)

JEFF:
Gosh you're cheesy. What?
Well, I'm gonna go. Just gotta…
but I'll see you tomorrow, right?

> (JEROME *nods.*

*JEFF stands, steps toward him, and,
hesitating, kisses him goodbye.)*

It's not the kind of kiss I'd ever want:
I feel it come and go before it starts,
his lips so tight with tension that I can't
feel him behind them, let alone the ~~love~~

part

of him you're kissing. Strangers suddenly,
no history to hold us in our touch.
I want to say *Don't go. It's done,* and be
contented, maybe, having said as much,

(They hug briefly.)

but my throat is sore, my mouth as dry as ice.
Somehow I stand there, ~~silent~~

breaking his heart twice.

*(As the door closes behind JEFF,
the stage begins to rotate, revealing
a hall, then another room on the
opposite side of the wall. JEROME
opens his bedroom door and the
fireflies swarm the hallway, then
follow him to his parents' bedroom,
where the couple lay reading in bed.*

*JEROME knocks on the door. The
lights again fade. Except for the
fireflies: they flood the unlit room
until the lights rise.)*

JEROME:
But I just stood there, breaking his heart twice

while he walked out, my present in his hand.
I want to call him and apologize, but…

MOM:
Well tell him that. I'm sure he'll understand.

JEROME:
I guess, but you don't know him like I do.
He acts all tough, but really he's… well… not.
Besides, I feel there's something here to prove,
like he should call me first. Is that a lot
to ask? I mean, I love him, but come on.
The least that he could do is maybe call
and, well, be nicer. I don't know. I'm done
feeling like crap when none of it's my fault.

DAD:
Well if you love him, and I know you do,
that seems to me the harder thing to lose.

> *(The fireflies scatter from the stage,
> forming loose constellations above
> the audience.)*

> *(SCENE: A Nightmare:*

> *The stage is dark when* JEROME
> *walks to the edge. Soon it is lit as
> if by moonlight. A single beam cuts
> sharply through onto the bedside
> table, making the edge of a phone
> just visible.* JEROME *sits at the
> edge of the bed.)*

It seems to me the hardest thing to lose
is loss itself. No matter what I try,
it will not leave me lossless.

>   (JEROME *nods puts his legs*
>   *beneath the covers.* JEFF *walks in,*
>   *but not into the light. He steps up to*
>   JEROME *for a kiss. But where are*
>   *the fireflies?*)

I refuse
to be the one forever left behind—
be it a boy who takes his touch away,
be it a shape I never knew was bliss:

>   (JEROME *kisses* JEFF.)

I pull my tired arms from around his waist,
and find them hanging empty without his
tangled there too. Unraveling from our source—
What source is that? Unbound, unbent. I gave
my answer to the ghost.

>   (JEFF *fades as if he had always been*
>   *a shadow.*)

He said to force
his love is not to love him truly, bravely.
And as I woke the room around me broke.
There was no mouth, but it was you who spoke.

(JEROME *reaches for the phone.*
Blackout.)

(SCENE.)

It was your mouth but it was her who spoke:
you said you couldn't talk so late. I knew
she sat there, listening, ~~amused~~
                    ~~and you~~
            and me, your joke—

            (JEROME *puts the receiver to his*
            chest, then lifts it back to his ear.)

I said goodnight, unsatisfied. ~~But you…~~

        (*He hangs up.*)

                It goes
like this: first heart, then touch, then fever breaks.
So that when I'm left alone with you, I wonder
when are we actually alone? For the sake
of ~~argument~~
            honesty, let's say whose spell you're under:
It's simple how she does it, turns on me,
as if I made you how you are, as if
I turned some switch and lit the fire, free
of consequences: catching tongue and lip.
(*Again, the stage rotates, this time revealing* JEFF'S *house.*
He sits at a table with MOTHER. *She smokes while he*
plays chords on his new guitar.)

It hurts to see ~~the difference~~

their reasoning, I guess.
To hear your parents say they know what's best.

(As the curtain is lowered, one can hear JEROME *shut his bedroom door. The music continues long after the houselights have come on.)*

INTERMISSION

ACT 2

> *(Before the curtain is lifted or the houselights signal a return, one can hear* JEROME *from backstage.)*

JEROME:

I heard your parents say they know what's best,
but Kyle, they don't. And even if you claim
you don't buy into what they're saying—

> *(The audience members quietly, awkwardly, find their seats. The houselights fade.)*
>
> Yes,

it's true. My parents smothered me. But blame's
a stupid waste of time. I'm telling you.
Who cares whose fault is whose, or even why?
Half the time it's messy and the truth

will get you nowhere, so don't waste your time—
I'm sorry, but it's true. And your folks
may think they're right, but you can't safely say
their love is half as great as ours. No jokes.
I'm serious. Don't look at me that way.
It's just that if you're happy, why's it matter?
And they'll get over it, at least they better.

(The curtain rises.)

> *(JEROME walks onstage. A*
> *spotlight follows him as he finds his*
> *seat. The edges of his surroundings*
> *are gilt by the amber light.)*

~~And they'll~~ get over it. ~~At least they better.~~
But I'll   I always do.

> *(A little more of his surroundings are*
> *revealed: rows of desks, all empty.)*

~~Alone~~ in ~~my~~ room,
A kid   a   I watch the teacher teach,
but can't pretend to hear her. Test of truth,
test of sweetness in the soil. I reach
in my bag and find your card once more, and read
it slow, in case I missed some subtle cure.

> *(JEROME reaches into his*
> *backpack with both hands, and*
> *when he pulls them out, they are*
> *clasped together. A faint light held*
> *between his palms.)*

Again, I feel I'm forcing you: your sea
the voice in every shell, your romance more
than the sum of its parts. Forgive me for my needs;
my clinginess is more than I can tame.
~~My breath still held~~
~~Your voice:~~

> *(When* JEROME *opens his hands,*
> *he reveals a single firefly. Freed,*
> *it remains in his hand, the light*
> *pulsing.)*

That ringing bell, it punctuates the scene,
but it's not time itself, not by that name.
I wondered at the love left in us all;
I saw us, each, who wander, hall to hall.

> *(As* JEROME *stands, the stage*
> *begins to rotate. The firefly remains*
> *calm in his cupped palm. He walks*
> *to a door, dreamily. He steps through*
> *it. On the other side, we see* JEFF
> *and his family waiting at a table.*
> *When* JEROME *closes the door*
> *behind him, the stage lights brighten*
> *suddenly. The family looks up.*
>
> JEROME *puts his backpack down*
> *and awkwardly takes an empty*
> *seat.)*

The only thing that's worse than coming late

is barely being noticed at the table.
I push the peas in circles on my plate,
wishing we weren't just sitting, watching cable.

> (JEFF'S STEPFATHER *tries*
> *repeatedly to change the channel*
> *during commercials, but the*
> *television doesn't respond to the*
> *remote.)*

JEFF'S STEPFATHER:
Why isn't the clicker working?

JEFF'S MOTHER:
Did you check the batteries, Hal?

> *(Eventually the show comes back*
> *on and he is content again.* JEFF'S
> MOTHER *doesn't look up from*
> *her plate;* JEFF *smiles at* JEROME
> *occasionally, but mostly watches the*
> *show.)*

But why the silence? Why the blunt refusal
to look me in the eyes, to ask a question?
I sit and ~~wonder~~
              study them—like why'd she choose Hal
if he won't give her what she needs? A lesson
for me: if Jeff can't ~~give me~~
              ~~tell me~~
                    show me what I need,
how long should I hold on to habit's love—
if I can't say with certainty it's me

he loves? But habit only. It's not enough
to love him; I need more than constancy:
I need to know he knows that he needs me.

> (JEROME *smiles uncomfortably,*
> *then stands. Only* JEFF *seems to*
> *notice. The boys walk to* JEFF's
> *room as the stage rotates, revealing*
> *it. The parents finish their dinner as*
> *they disappear into the darkness.)*

> (*The two stand quietly.* JEFF *sits*
> *on the bed, but* JEROME *doesn't*
> *follow him.)*

I wonder at the love left in us all:
I move the papers, touch the photographs,
and wonder what is left—if ~~nights like this~~
                              I should fall
or catch me while I can. How much is left
~~and do I hold it all~~
and is there love for me in you, addressed
and ready to pour out—is it pouring now?
Is this all I get?

> (JEROME *turns his back to* JEFF,
> *pretends to look at a the pictures in*
> *a* SEVEN WONDERS OF THE
> WORLD *wall calendar.)*

Are you the best
there is for me? Is what I want ~~to know~~
                              ~~a show~~
                              a tower

in a field? More love than enough? Are you ~~here~~

                                           hearing

me?

JEFF:
Jerry—what's wrong?
You've been weird since dinner.

            A statue where some broken body stood?

JEFF:
Jerry? Come on.

JEROME:
I didn't know your Dad would buy us beer.

JEFF:
Pretty cool, huh? Since it's a special occasion and all.

                     (JEFF stands and steps toward
                     JEROME, *who pushes him away.)*

JEROME:
You mean you told them?! How'd they take it? Good?

JEFF:
Dude. I told you. They've known
longer than I have. They'll just need some time
getting used to it. Not all parents are
cheerleaders for gayness.

JEROME:
I can't believe you'd say that. And tonight!

I mean what a gesture: how 'bout start a fight?!

JEFF:
Okay, Jerry. What is this really about?

> *(JEFF tries again to hug JEROME.*
> *He tries to push him off, but JEFF*
> *won't let him.)*

I want the gesture—momentary ~~hand~~
                              stroke
~~of hand in mine~~
I want to see the pulleys and the cords,
that lavishly wild machine of love, bespoke,
~~mined~~
made mine by longing. And you: severely bored.

> *(JEROME begins to explain.)*

How can you say you love me—do you really?—
when you can't ~~shoulder~~
                    show her, wholly, who I am?
Unbridled scope or scale, ~~unbroken trellis~~
                              the kind of feeling
you can't just ~~say~~
                write without disturbing the calm
~~of a blank page~~
~~of sense.~~
You think I speak like this because I can?
~~Because without the beat there is no heart?!~~
My form is not my structure, it's my mode:
it's how I handle ~~love~~
                    truth; it's how I ~~find it~~

land

squarely inside ~~the~~ self,

                my   honestly ~~wrote~~

                             ~~wrought~~

                             ~~written~~

                              found!

It isn't that I long for you to sing,
it's that I long for care in everything.

Because without the beat, there is no heart.
And sentiments seem strung along on lines
of half-felt courtesies—when what I want
is romance strung upon a blooming vine—
not for the flowers, but for their opening.
In love, any truth is kind because it's ~~true~~

                            real.

And any lie is worse ~~because it's not~~.

                    I hope you sing—

but not because you think I want you to.
Because you can't hold back, so much unsaid,
because you've looked so deeply in my eyes
that you can't see much else. Because instead
of wanting your life the same, you realize
that maybe it can never be again!
~~And that's okay.~~

                    (JEFF nods, but JEROME shakes
                    his head no.)

JEROME:
Remember how you said we should stay friends—

JEFF:

Okay, now you're just pissing me off!

Are you even interested in giving me a chance?

Has it occurred to you that maybe this is all

harder for me than it is for you? I mean,

I'm trying to be romantic. I gave you that stupid card

because it was in iambic pentameter on the front

or whatever. I thought you'd think it was funny.

*(The two stand there in silence for
several moments.)*

JEFF:

Well, this was supposed to be a surprise,

but I don't know how to even bring it up.

I tried to write you a song or whatever.

But it's really stupid. I mean REALLY.

*(JEFF goes to his closet and pulls
out the guitar. He sits next to
JEROME and begins to play
the chords. He clears his throat.
JEROME laughs a little, though
he is already crying. JEFF gets to
the part of the song where he should
begin singing, but chickens out.
He begins the intro again. On the
second try, he begins singing.)*

JEFF:

Remember when I said we should stay friends

Because I didn't want to say goodbye.

I take it back; I simply can't pretend

A friendship holds as much as you and I

Hold daily: holding hands or holding still,
Holding each other late into the night—

> *(As he sings, the fireflies in the*
> *audience return to the stage. They*
> *form a bright cloud above the song.)*

Or holding tight, so patiently, until
That moment we're together, the timing right…

So I'm not as good at metaphors as you,
Or saying often that I love you still
But you know what I'm saying when I do…

Whisper in your ear or tell you softly,
Even if what I'm saying isn't poetry
And I mess up everything, just like me.

> *(JEROME laughs louder, wiping*
> *his face.)*

My songs are quiet, wordless rants at best,
because I'm scared to lose all that we've made.
And so I hold my cards close to my chest
and question every bet, each pair I've played.

So I'm not as good at metaphors as you,

> *(JEFF's voice cracks a little and they*
> *both laugh. JEFF rolls his eyes.)*

Or singing, even. How embarrassing.
But you know what I'm saying when I do…

Whisper in your ear or tell you, my voice cracking,
Even if what I'm saying isn't poetry
And I mess up everything, and it isn't perfect. And I'm
sorry.

> *(The lights fade as the boys embrace.
> The fireflies surround them, so
> brightly the audience must look
> away. When they look back, the
> couple is gone.)*

JEROME:
Don't be.

JEFF:
Happy anniversary Jerome.

> *(SCENE: A voice. Who knows
> which? The curtain is lowered slowly.
> Some chords begin. The audience
> remains in their seats after the
> houselights have come on.)*

I'll never know what love is like for you,
how much or little you have found in it,
or if, one morning, we might learn some truth
and let it break this spell we wrestle with—
as some astonished child would do, his heart
still easy to unset, his mind made up
as soon as it's unmade: ~~his parent's part~~
his parents having parted,
~~placed their bets.~~

Some day some force may come and interrupt
what calm we've ~~found~~
                      made, but I can't worry now
about the end, still busy with beginning.
I see us through new eyes and wonder how
it is we have such lasting. ~~We're on a roll.~~
                         My God, we're winning!
The boy I was wants only to ~~find~~ love,
                    make
to know it's real and realize that's enough.

(THE END)

Jay Michaelson

Foreign Thoughts

I don't feel ashamed
when I spy you at the mikva,
out of the corner of my eye—
a body is a body,
and wants what it wants.

And I don't feel I'm intruding
if, when you're dancing in the synagogue,
I glimpse a swatch of exposed flesh
while you circle and sway—
there is no harm in these idle glances;
just nature, following itself.

But when I turn back and see you davening,
when I behold the contortions of your face,
as you plead ad yearn,
then I am abashed.
Then I am guilty, and then I beg forgiveness;
for trespassing what is private
and seeing hour holy
nakedness.

Please
let me not transgress this boundary
unwanted.

Miguel Murphy

Self-Portrait's Caravaggio Walking Night's Pier

How I love the head of a limp
        pink dollop, pursed
at the base of the groin, lip brown & reddish
another mouth ripe against death

& hard kissing, twilight's deceitful cherub.
        If men are erotic
at all, if undressing the rosy eclipse
of his nipple's silk-salmon

dare, if in his face a girl's laughter
wears the face of a boy, if he is shy
        horse, coy
yellow curl fallen down on bare shoulder

then be wedded. Boys who love boys
        damasked with bluish
hats, darkened like bruises & fruit pits
sulk under the Santa Monica Pier, crossing

as over breastplates their arms, for warmth,
posing secure, leaning in, half-
concealed against night's wall—Desire
brings them here. It brings me, & others who fail

our own sex. My little brother says, *that's gay*
meaning "stupid," "retarded," "illogical," "broken,"
"gaudy," & "other," but he says *that*
doesn't mean *me*. I think I should tell him

how it does, how it's thumb is on
my thigh's purple sore, so knuckling
        a wound with its
crooked word, its world, its squash-yellow

malignant turning. Here underneath
filial dirt & glitter
chattering upon the pier, the *celestia* of carnival rides
is simulating mechanical disaster, & some boys

 flee their families, searching beach wood
& the view abandoned of sunsets where now
        hot moon pools
in the footsteps, the sand gutted

where a heel balled in. To admit
to coming like they do, with the masculine
        image of the dog-god
biting into them, is impossible. Instead

they stop to tie a shoelace. Glance at nothing,
in *its* direction, as if waiting
        for the one who should have appeared
by now. Ironically, touching arrows

on his wrist, ticking away, feigning
impatience, here is a young one alone intoxicatingly
seeking approval from the unannounced.
His eyes flash iridescent

wingfly. As they turn away, peering
into other smudges of darkness where older
        men wait hungrily, they beg. One older
one who does not look away, stares hawkish

hooking this young one supple
with need, demanding the very skin to flourish
magnetically, tendering, waxing aromatic, the boy-skin's
movement chilled & blushing, until the apple

curl of a lip slips off the man. Because he knows
he will not be refused. The body wants to
want to be changed, scoured, stripped, turned in-
side out with pleasure, though the boy

doesn't know yet how. So he risks it.
This cobalt shredding
          distance with its panic & salty
ravishments. Behind them. The ocean

loud with wars. One boy
searches the grape-dark face of a man
heralded by seagulls
like messengers of Always piercing

stars out with their slick black knives. This older
one with his stare
penetrates the invisible. Plum. Stone. Maturity:
Here is the fruit of your longing

shriveled like a goat's black tongue. Not caring, but
not knowing yet the consequences to offering
          himself to morning's indifferent
man who will use him this night, rabid in-

vulnerability,
the younger one presses forward, leaning in

on one foot like a promise
made accidentally
to fall, to lose, to love,

to close his eyes against a man's warm fur
tripped with violet—this man watching from above
waiting for it to happen—this boy bearing down
insinuation's musky shadow

to taste & give up everything.

Billeh Nickerson

The Ultra Centrifuge

When I asked my lover what he'd done that day
    I wanted him to ask me too
since I'd just bought groceries and felt really
proud,
    but instead of the usual summations,
the subsequent kiss, he just stood there, told me,
    he spun people's blood all day,

tube after tube in the ultra centrifuge.
    I'd never heard of a centrifuge before
but I liked it sound so while my lover explained
    how it spins fast enough to make HIV
separate from plasma like cream gathering atop
    an old fashioned milk bottle

I practiced pronouncing it the same way
    I repeat the names to foreign places
in case I ever go there: ul-tra cen-tri-fuge,
    ultra centrifuge, ultra centrifuge spinning
inside my mouth, my tongue separating
    each word by syllabic weight.

My lover said it's easy when you don't know
    their faces, when you don't see them
exit the clinic doors with Band-Aids
    on short-sleeved arms, when you can't feel
the warmth of their just given blood
    through your latex gloves and glass tubes.

That evening while my lover lay beside me
    I wondered how it felt
to hold the blood between his fingers,
    whether he learned to hold
my cock from holding test tubes
    or test tubes from my cock.

Christopher Nield

What It's Like, After All

I have discovered love;
You weren't what I expected.
Your paunch, for example,
Isn't – let's be honest –
The ideal.
And yet I have found rest on it.
Just touching it –
That unfettered belly,
That soft underside
Of your adamantine suit –
Is utter joy –
Cold fluttering lightness.

I have discovered faith
In your folds, those august
Fistfuls of too-muchness,
That smooth interior
All over, all over!
My caramel, sheer, irresistible Ganesha.

I have discovered lust
In your feet,
Those fascinated dainty snubs at which far point your
    body ends
And curves up to begin
All over again.

I have discovered trust

In your technique:
Ten out of ten.

I have discovered home
In your grip,
The way you fashion me
With hands, so delectably unseen,
When you allow yourself
To quicken from prim majesty
And, afterwards, on my chest
You sleep. That fat, elusive
Upward flicker
Of grace
At your imperious mouth
Astounds me – agonises
My lank heart.

Peter Pereira

Sweat Equity

Layers of green shag smothered oak hardwoods,
rolls of 1950s newspapers insulated
a basement stairway closet, aluminum-framed
windows with broken seals grew greenish algae.

But how else could we look back now upon
romantic weekends scraping layers of paint,
lovers quarreling over colors for siding, then
hanging new double-hungs.

Re-roofing, re-plumbing, re-wiring,
removing a false lowered ceiling:
not so much a revision
as a retelling,

adding to what had gone before,
working up the sweet sweat
that makes a relationship hum,
makes a place indelibly, undeniably yours.

It's how we come to inhabit where we are:
tearing down a wall, planting a tree,
brushing another coat of paint onto plaster,
lowering a hedge to reclaim a view.

Like when we wrote our names
onto the closet wall of the first apartment
we shared, before repaneling it with cedar—
we're still there, beneath the surface, built in.

Carl Phillips

Night Song

Servitude. Conquest. The one who, from the hip, keeps
pushing himself up into the other's mouth. The one who
takes from behind. The more prismatic of the Roman
emperors—at each turn of the light, yet another shade

of a near-unstoppable will-to-power, of humiliation's
not-so-strange allure. Later, those emperors of the almost-
finished second century, who by their own example make
a case for submission to what resists control: Hadrian

falls for the boy Antinous; Marcus Aurelius for a stoicism
in the face of corruption, plague, barbarians...Conquest
and servitude; suffering, and suffering's famous ability
to bring about a patience that pleasure ultimately has little

time for. I close my eyes. I remain persuadable. I give
up what I can. Who's to say what will not be useful?

Kenneth Pobo

Unlearning

That creative writing prof I had sophomore year
who said Whitman wasn't gay
believed in universal poems. He meant
str8 poems. Only a str8 person could be universal
since most people fucked the other sex. OK,
I admit it, he didn't say fuck. He rarely said

what he meant. I knew I couldn't turn in
poems about my boyfriend
or charming high school dalliances I had,
mostly in daydreams. His wedding ring,
a classroom climate. It never got above
freezing unless you agreed with him.
He trotted out a poem he had in
Southern Wishbone Review, all about his kids.
My, my they did funny things. It took years

to pull his nails out of my brain. Whitman
helped pull them out, one by one. We swam
naked in a pond. The fact that he was dead
didn't bother me. In fact, it made him more lively.

We didn't fret about the universe. We packed it
a picnic lunch, sat by a froggy creek and talked
about our favorite poems.

Andy Quan

Lonely Planet

Land of smiles, the airport exhorts. Planes spit
out weary travellers, oxygen-starved, circadian
rhythms arrhythmic. Occasional gritty reports
do nothing to sate your friends' envy of business
junkets. You check in, achy and nauseous,
sleep clutching at more sleep. You wander
the crowded pavement, ask strangers' counsel until:
      EMAIL the sign shouts, the lone
terminal surprising you. He's sent you a letter,
compressed down into pulse and signal
reassembled in the corner of a random hotel lobby.

   It's about this separation; I find it hard to say.
   Can we discuss?

You've been stretching the idea of a long distance
relationship, a canvas over a frame but the scene
undecided: him in Canada, you usually in Australia,
now Bangkok.
                  He'll never know this
world but does it make a difference?
Beggars and tourists, tailors of custom-made
suits, windows filled with the finest
Thai silk, a parade of taxis in lemon, lime
and cherry chrome, a pack of motorcyclists idling
at the lights.
                  Alone and work burdened
you type

   This is just not the time.

      and stagger into the fetid afternoon—
sewage, charcoal, exhaust—step through
 vendors of wristwatches, sunglasses, CDs,
wooden curios, blackened skewers of chicken
and pork, durian, flower garlands ribboned in red.

He astonished you once by knowing when you
woke and slept halfway around the world.
Now: no redemption, this week is
the beginning of the end of everything.

Nearby, tuk-tuk drivers court passengers with
the promise of inside information. Stray dogs doze
smugly (Buddhists won't harm them, leave rice
on doorsteps.) At Wat Po, Buddha magnificently
reclines. Farther away: a Thai massage, an exotic
meal, a clever souvenir.
                    Small rewards,
but not necessarily the ones you were looking for.

Steven Reigns

Legal Pads

I met him online,
pressed in an e-mail for his number.
His confession followed.
Even if I had his number to dial,
he wouldn't be able to hear me
on the other end.

We soon found ways of contact
and would sit on my couch
having conversations
on legal pads.

It was on that lined paper I was told
of his Midwest childhood,
Gallaudet University,
rude waiters,
and the maddening bass at gay clubs.

After 3 dates and 4 filled notepads,
the hands with which he spoke to others explored my body.
Speaking with touch, not the pen,
tracing details I had long forgotten:
the circular scar on my shin,
the folds of my ear, and
my ticklish belly.
Through out it all I heard his sounds—
the deep primal uttering of excitement or fascination.

We'd see foreign films at a rundown theatre.
The poor sound system inconsequential
as we read each yellowed word at the screen's edge.
I became accustomed to a shaking bed waking me up,
a flickering light signifying company,
and no radio in the car.

He and I, out of necessity, scribed our desires
Each scrawled sentence purposeful and precise.

When he was not with me, I'd reread our legal pads.
Each line sealing my memory of that moment.
I reread the lines of his love for me,
something to reference later.
That his feeling was documented
felt more authentic, unshakeable,
almost unrefuted like
a legal document itself.

Shane Rhodes

His Hands Were Hounds Over Me

I think back to when we met. Our bodies were
younger then and sex moved through our cells
like the heat from an acid etch. It still brings me
to my knees. The only thing we didn't know of
love was the magnitude of its disappointment.
But I don't care anymore or, rather, believe
at one time I cared. Nowadays, I sit in bars
drinking beer as warm as the urine I pump out.
I talk often. I put money in the jukebox and
her him rolling down the narrow passage. I try
not to lose my head. I try to be with men who
are normal which means I spend much of the
night alone. I am so alone. I am torn asunder.
My head floats beneath the darkening water.

Jason Roush

Letter To Bill

First things: let me apologize
(a terrible way to begin, I realize)
for the delay in getting this to you.
Over fourteen years have passed,
but seeing as there's no time there,
I guess it isn't really such an issue.
Last night, flipping through a stack
of old letters, I came across my first
and only one from you, summer of '92,
the summer after I left school. I sat
on the floor beside the bed and read it
over and over again, finding delight
in the bit of your spirit in my hand,
on a page, when it hit me I was sitting
in exactly the same spot to which
I sank when Andy called to tell me
you were dead. An aneurysm,
a vessel burst inside your head—
not AIDS, which might have made
more sense, hovering as it did
above men of your generation.
Death doesn't like to make sense.
Refuses reason. No more worrying
about "the state of entropy" in
Mark's and Nissa's rooms: "After all
these years I have all of my kids
together again which is a pretty
nice feeling." With no choice but
to wait for a cheap airplane fare,

I missed the funeral by three weeks.
Sammy, of course, was a total mess
when I saw him. I stuck my head
into his office, and just a glance
up at me was enough to reduce him
to tears. (How to steer away from
sentiment here?) Telling me how he
hadn't set foot in the house since
he'd found you lying naked across
the tiles, the shower still running.
I visited your gravesite at Hiram
Cemetery, a rolling square of land
you share with plots dating back as far
as the Civil War. At that point, yours
was nothing more than a small mound
of dirt heaped with dead flowers. I sat
on a pile of rocks nearby, took in gelid
April light, the clarity of an unbridled
Ohio sky. I threw a fist at it, silently
kicked at roots of trees too old and
stubborn to be moved. A dry wind
sighed in their branches, a song.
You didn't want to be buried there,
beside that winding stretch of rural
highway. Judging from your letter,
you'd be better off and certainly more
satisfied scattered off the coast of
Provincetown ("magical, I hope you
and Michael have gotten out there"),
or even somewhere inside that bar
you loved in Montreal, the one with
"stunning" strippers ("Some even have
erections!"). I never said you were

a moralist. But yes. Your love for
the body, teaching your students and me
the infinite dangers of it: "Remember
safe sex," your letter's final piece
of sage advice. Old courage-teacher,
professor of biology and dignity,
I rested a stone on your unfinished
grave, blessed the ground in which they
placed you, and the world started
teaching itself to me. Fondly,

Jason Schneiderman

Self Portrait of the Artist as a Young Sex Object (Age 19)

It was a nice body, slender,
not as flexible as you might
have hoped, fun for a few hours,
but nothing you would want
to keep or hold onto. The bodies
of young men are like
furniture from Ikea,
clean lines, smooth surfaces,
but no real promise
of longevity or staying power
and mine was no different,
and I knew that, which was
why I wanted the bodies
of older men, their skin
mapping out the place
I would go, their touch
the promise of living
into that country of age that
seemed so far away that
I thought might never get there.
One man would tell me
nothing, except to confirm
that he was older than
my father, and this was
on the subway, the morning
after we had lain down
on his bed under a painting

of him that had been done
when he was still a model,
decades ago. He liked
my body because it reminded
him of the one he had lost.
And it comforted him,
because his had been
so much prettier.

Gregg Shapiro

Billy

Your father taught you how to drink beer. How to flare
your nostrils, sustain a belch for almost thirty seconds.
He taught me how to ride a bicycle when my own father
was too busy stacking grapefruits in the produce department
at Hillman's Fine Foods. The teachers couldn't teach you,
so they tried to hold you back, restrain you like a wildfire.
They calmed you, temporarily, in their pastel rooms, in the long,

flat, red-bricked school. Outside, you changed colors, burned
brighter, gleamed like the straw blond hair on your head. You
only pretended to laugh. Mesmerized by your turbulent behavior,
I clung to you like sweat. Fascinated, infatuated. Bored with
the children of my mother's friends, who were as delicate as glass
and chipped with a sharp look. I dreamed you were a hammer
and we shattered them, left them for their fractured parents

to reassemble and glue. Your grandmother's second husband
drove a cab in the city. When he came home, he'd drive us
around in his red Rambler. Your brothers, my brother, came
along, sat in the front seat. We sat in the back, sealing our fate
with blood and spit. Making promises that we knew we'd never
keep. I couldn't bounce a basketball, swing a bat, catch a football.
You made it seem so easy, effortless, natural, as if you were born

wearing spikes and a catcher's mitt. In all the games we played,
I was the weaker sex, even though we were all boys. In order
to win your affection, I needed to find a sport that made us all
equals and didn't reward its victors. The first time we had sex

was in your parents' bed. A dog-eared copy of "Open Marriage" was on the headboard and I opened my mouth to swallow yours. The bed was expansive, lumpy, concave. You were smooth, playful,

curious. The sheets no longer smelled of your mother's Final Net hairspray, your father's cigarettes and Old Spice cologne. We were addicted instantly, hooked for what seemed like a lifetime to a habit that was unkickable, a thirst unquenchable. In between, we rode our bicycles into the city, swam in the heavily chlorinated water at Oakton Pool. I cheered from the sidelines at your athletic prowess. I, who gave you your first cigarette, your first kiss.

Reginald Shepherd

All of This and Nothing

As if there were nothing,
or nothing but this: you looking away
again, embarrassed by noon
or the sound of my voice:
as if we had been lovers,
or could have spoken to each other
openly. On days like this light seems a poor excuse,
marking your face as you drive
me home, marking and measuring the struts
of the bridge. White buildings
of a city I intend to leave
make promises they mean not to keep,
but we move toward them
anyway. Too many things
I should have known, or realized I knew, things
to know better than: the shadows
lining your hands, shadows bisecting
your face. Look: that line beneath the water
is pure quartz. Why should you
care? The light shifts
with a sudden swerve of the wheel:
we're almost there.
I let the day do what it must.
As if it were all
equal to this, a car backing into
a one-way street.

D. Antwan Stewart

Elegy

for Jeremy Spring

Each day I spin yarns around my heart.
Lulled to sleep with no body to warm

me, not even a dint in the mattress hints
I've missed a thousand habitual nights of coupling.

If the days weren't so filled with birds'
quick-beat flapping, I may have forgotten the quieter

tenor of fish leaping, flopping mid-air at sea, how
this is the way in which surviving the dead becomes an act

of unkindness. Nodding politely to the woman
carrying her child on hip, I must admit the world does,

indeed, continue to revolve: the moon
cycles and tides excavate rubble, washes it

ashore, I know, just as I know dinner for two
is too much dinner for one. Half the equation is missing—

though my memory of you survives:
you sunning yourself those afternoons hoping

if you perspired the toxins would scatter like a flock of crows.
This is how I like to remember you—

not the mattress worn smooth, nor the dishes filling the cabinet
with dust. But the sun ravaging you with light,

those birds lost somewhere in your body's cast shadow.

Scott Wiggerman

The Interview Date

Where are you from?

What I wanted
was to watch you speak,
see the pink raft of tongue
lap at your lips,
the beacon of Adam's apple,
beckon up and down.

How long have you lived here?

What I wanted
was to watch you lean in,
observe the swells of hair
eddying from your shirt,
the surge of nipples,
hard as a rocky coast.

Where did you go to school?

What I wanted
was to watch you stand,
gauge the strain of your anchor,
note the cove of buttocks,
lean as the Strait of Gibraltar,
a tight figure-eight.

What do you do for fun?

What I wanted
was to leave the coffeeshop,
shuck you like an oyster,
raise your mast,
unfurl your sails,
ride you into the night—

but that would wait
till the second date.

Gregory Woods

Telemachus

I had a reputation on the playing fields of Harrow
For making an advantage of what should have caused me sorrow.
When bullied for my foot or complimented as a fairy,

I never let it pass but gave a master-class in fury—
For whence but from a schoolboy's ardour lead the paths of glory?
Renowned not only for a temper but a heart as fiery

As Strómboli, I started to be figured for a hero,
Diminutive but worth the courting. I was never surer
Of love than in that season of aggression, never nearer

Reciprocating kiss for kiss, devouree for devourer.
While every boy in my embrace became a doe-eyed houri,
My pallet vied with the divans of Isfahan and Cairo.

This tongue was never hindered by so much as a caesura:
Each friend elicited a flood of love, like Petrarch's Laura,
Until his moment passed and Mother Nature made him hairy.

Emmanuel Xavier

A Simple Poem

I want you to continue writing
because I will not always be around

With lips that will never touch mine
read your poems out loud
so that the words are left engraved on the wall
make me feel your voice rush through me
like a breeze from Oyá

I want to hear about Puerto Rico
about sisters with names like La Bruja
about educating youth about AIDS
I want to hear about life in the Boogie Down Bronx
surviving on the Down Low
don't leave out stories about men
you have loved and still love

I want you to write poems that you will never read
press hard on the paper so that the ink runs deep
hold the pen tight so that you control the details
prove to me that I inspire you
reveal yourself between the lines
hear my praise with each flicker of the candle
Write a poem for me

Do not choose a fresh page from a brand new journal
use paper that has been crumbled and tossed
thrown out by a spineless father only to be recycled
Save a tree for future poets to write under

Rewrite me into someone more attractive
stronger than life has made me
make me tough and sexy, aggressive like a tiger
stain the pages with cum, lube, the arousal you find
at the sight of naked boys, draw me sketches
bring the words to life with images
make me a man with this poem

Read it in front of the audience
with hidden messages just for me
be real and tell me why
I am only worth a haiku

Your epics are meant for others
I already know,
use red ink to match the blood from these wounds
with brutal honesty
let me die with your last sentence

Then resurrect me with rhyme
read from your gut
let me hear the wisdom of *mi abuelo* in your voice
let me find my father in you
remind me of all the men that left me broken promises

In your eyes I want to see a poem
when you bring me to tears
with painful memories
buried beneath your thick skin

Between teeth gapped like divas,
I want to hear quotes from books
I never read

Make me believe you want to be a poet

Make my heart break,
tell me why you could never love me
with just a few words
leave me lost and insecure
feel the admiration of others
bask in their desire
forget that I am there

Pound your fists in the air with passion
go off about politics, poverty, machismo and hate
scream poems that don't give a fuck
about traditions, slamming or scores
save your whispers for those who make love to you

Write a poem for me that makes me want to puff a joint

A poem that loses control
unafraid to be vulnerable
for once just make me believe
it is all worth letting go
when the smoke clears
I will understand
the reason
I am just another face
in the crowd

I want you to continue writing
because I will not always be around

C. Dale Young

The Second Omen: Spring

One refuses to hold the other's hand.
One pours wine and misses the glass.
Signs sent by a lesser god again and again
to no avail. That the body is mostly water,

this we could agree upon. All else was less
than palatable. I said I loved you, too.
In this way, the heart lies, too.
The dogwoods bloom; their lies, like mine,

gorgeous and capable of seduction.
And outside, the vines kept twisting and twisting…
Yes, outside, the vines kept twisting and twisting,
gorgeous and capable of seduction.

The dogwood's blooms are lies like mine.
In this way, the heart lies, too.
Palatable? I said I loved you, too.
This we could agree upon. All else was less,

to no avail. The body is still mostly water.
Signs. Lesser gods. Again and again,
one pours wine and misses the glass,
one refuses to hold the other's hand.

ABOUT THE POETS

Antler, former poet laureate of Milwaukee, is author of *Factory, Last Words, Selected Poems, Open Bible With a Gun On It, Exclamation Points Ad Infinitum!, Deathrattles vs. Comecries,* and *Ever-Expanding Wilderness.* Winner of the Walt Whitman Award, a Pushcart Prize and the Witter Bynner Prize from the American Academy & Institute of Arts & Letters in New York City, his gay poems appear in many anthologies including *Gay & Lesbian Poetry in in Our Time; Gay Roots; Son of the Male Muse; Eros in Boystown; The Badboy Book of Erotic Poetry; A Day for a Lay: A Century of Gay Poetry; Between the Cracks: A Daedalus Anthology of Kinky Verse; First Person Sexual; I Do/I Don't; Men of Our Time; To Be a Man; Erotic by Nature; Reclaiming the Heartland: Lesbian & Gay Voices from the Midwest.*

Rane Arroyo is a gay, Puerto Rican, Midwestern poet and playwright. In 2008-09, he will have published 9 books of poems, including *The Buried Sea: New & Selected Poems.* He has won an Ohio Excellence Artist Award, the John Ciardi Prize, The Carl Sandburg Poetry Prize, the Stonewall Books Prize, among many other honors. His work has appeared in over twenty anthologies and has had plays performed throughout the United States and a few international stages. He is working on his memoirs and a book of gay poems, *Sin Santos.*

John Barton has published eight books of poetry and five chapbooks, including *Designs from the Interior, Sweet Ellipsis, Hypothesis* and *Asymmetries*. A bilingual edition of his third book, *West of Darkness: Emily Carr, a self-portrait, released* in 2006. He is co-editor (with Billeh Nickerson) of Seminal: *The Anthology of Canada's Gay Male Poets*. He has won three Archibald Lampman Awards, a Patricia Hackett Prize (University of Western Ontario), an Ottawa Book Award, and a CBC Literary Award. He lives in Victoria, where he edits *Th e Malahat Review*.

Dan Bellm is a poet and translator living in San Francisco. He has published three collections of poetry, *One Hand on the Wheel, Buried Treasure*, and, most recently, *Practice*. His poems have appeared in *Poetry, Ploughshares, The Threepenny Review, The Best American Spiritual Writing*, and *Word of Mouth: an Anthology of Gay American Poetry*. His translations of poetry and fiction from Spanish have appeared in many journals and anthologies. His translation of *The Legend of the Wandering King*, a novel by Laura Gallego García, made the American Library Association's Notable Books for Children list and the *School Library Journal's* Outstanding International Books list for 2006.

David Bergman is the author of three books of poetry, the most recent of which is *Heroic Measures*. *Crccking the Code*, his first book, won the George Elliston Prize. He is also the author of two critical studies, *Gaiety Transfigured* and *The Violet Hour: The Violet Quill and the Making of Gay Culture*. He won a Lambda Literary Award for best anthology for *Men on Men 2000*. He teaches at Towson University in Maryland.

Jericho Brown's poems have appeared or are forthcoming in *Callaloo, Prairie Schooner, Pleiades, jubilat, New England Review, Barrow Street, AGNI Online*, and *Post Road,* among other journals. His collection *Please released* from Western Michigan University's New Issues Poetry & Prose. He has a Ph.D. in Creative Writing and Literature from the University of Houston and an M.F.A. from the University of New Orleans, and is currently an Assistant Professor at the University of San Diego.

James Cihlar's first book of poems, *Undoing,* was published by Little Pear Press in 2008. His poems have appeared in *Prairie Schooner, Bloom, Minnesota Monthly, Northeast, The James White Review, Wisconsin River Valley Journal, Water-Stone Review, Briar Cliff Review, Plain Songs,* and in the anthology *Aunties.* He has won awards from the Minnesota State Arts Board and the Academy of American Poets and has a Ph.D. from the University of Nebraska. He has taught at the University of Wisconsin in Stevens Point as well as at the University of Minnesota in Minneapolis. He is currently the managing editor for Milkweed Editions.

Jeffery Conway is the author of *Phoebe 2002: An Essay in Verse* and *The Album That Changed My Life*, a finalist for the Lambda Literary Award. He lives in New York City.

Steven Cordova's first book of poems, *Long Distance*, is forthcoming from Bilingual Press. He is author of the chapbook Slow Dissolve. His poems have appeared in *Barrow Street, Calalloo, The Journal* and *Northwest Review*, among other journals and magazines, as well as the anthologies *The Winds Shifts* and *Ravishing DisUnities: Real Ghazals in English*.

Jeff Crandall is a Seattle poet, glass artist and a founding editor of Floating Bridge Press. His work has appeared previously in *Atlanta Review, Beloit Poetry Journal, Bloom, The Gay & Lesbian Review, JAMA,* and *Seattle Review* among others. His book of poems, *The Grief Pool* was published by Firestorm Press.

James Crews holds an M.F.A. in Poetry from the University of Wisconsin-Madison. His work has appeared or is forthcoming in *Prairie Schooner, Alimentum, Best New Poets 2006,* and *Fourteen Hills,* among others. A chapbook, *Small Yellow Envelopes: A Poem after Felix Gonzalez-Torres* is scheduled to appear next year from Parallel Press. He currently lives with his partner in Humboldt County, California.

Brian Cronwall is Assistant Professor of English at Kaua'I Community College in Hawai'i. His poems have appeared in numerous journals and anthologies in Hawai'i, mainland United States, Guam, Australia, Japan, United Kingdom, and France.

Steve Fellner's debut book of poems Blind Date with Cavafy won the 2006 Marsh Hawk Poetry Press Prize and the 2008 Thom Gunn Gay Male Poetry Award. He teaches at SUNY Brockport.

John Frazier is a poet and teacher. his work has been published in the *Massachusetts Review, Antioch Review, The New Republic*, and many other journals and publications. He writes sonnets, aubades, and other formalist poems.

Brad Gooch's biography of Flannery O'Connor will be published by Little, Brown in 2009. He has been awarded a Guggenheim fellowship and a National Endowment for the Humanities fellowship, and is the author of a book of poems, a book of stories, three novels, two books of memoir/self-help, and *City Poet*, a biography of Frank O'Hara. He lives in New York City.

Jeremy Halinen is coeditor and cofounder of *Knockout*. He has a M.F.A. from Eastern Washington University. His chapbook *Fragments of Water* won the Alan Bunn Memorial Award. Recent poems appear or are forthcoming in *Dos Passos Review*, *Gertrude*, *Pontoon 10*, *Quarter After Eight*, *Rio Grande Review*, and the *2008 Outside Voices Anthology of Younger Poets*.

James Allen Hall's first book of poems, *Now You're the Enemy*, was a finalist for the Walt Whitman Award from the Academy of American Poets and won the University of Arkansas Poetry Series prize. He has published poems in numerous journals, including TriQuarterly, Boston Review, Alaska Quarterly Review, Third Coast, West Branch, the James White Review, Redivider, and others. He has a Ph.D. in Creative Writing and Literature from the University of Houston and an M.F.A. from Bennington College, and teaches creative writing at the State University of New York at Potsdam.

Forrest Hamer is the author of three books of poetry: *Call & Response*, *Middle Ear*, and *Rift*. Much of his writing deals with his experiences growing up as an African American.

Reginald Harris is the author of one book of poems, *10 Tongues, a* finalist for a Lambda Literary Award and the ForeWord Book of the Year. A fellow of Cave Canem: African American Poetry Workshop/Retreat (cavecanempoets.org), his poetry, fiction, reviews, and articles have appeared in a variety of journals and websites, including *African-American Review, Black Issues Book Review, Poetry Midwest,* and *Sou'wester* and in the anthologies *Best Black Gay Erotica, Bum Rush the Page, The Ringing Ear: Black Poets Lean South,* and *Voices Rising: Celebrating 20 Years of Black Lesbian, Gay, Bisexual and Transgender Writing.*

Sean Horlor was born in Edmonton. His work has been published widely in such journals as Arc, Event, The Fiddlehead, Grain, Pine Magazine, The Claremont Review, Inner Harbour Review, and The Malahat Review. His poem "In Praise of Beauty" win first place in *THIS Magazine*'s 2006 Great Canadian Literary Hunt. His first collection of poetry, *Made Beautiful by Use released in 2007.* He currently lives in Vancouver.

Richard Johns grew up in Chicago and now lives, with his boyfriend of many years, in a small town on the far western fringe of that lovely city's metropolitan sprawl. He has had poems published in *The Spoon River Quarterly, Strong Coffee, After Hours, Chicagopoetry.com,* and *MiPoesias.* Three widely unavailable chapbooks bear his name: *2000 Poems, Hollywood Beach,* and *Explicit Lyrics: Poems.*

Jee Leong Koh was born in Singapore, read English at Oxford University, and completed his Creative Writing M.F.A. at Sarah Lawrence College. His poems have appeared in Singaporean anthologies, and in American and

British journals such as *Crab Orchard Review, The Ledge Magazine, Gay & Lesbian Review Worldwide*, and *Mimesis*. He is the author of *Payday Loans*. His new book of poems *Equal to the Earth* is forthcoming from Poets Wear Prada Press in 2009. He lives in New York City, and blogs at jeeleong.blogspot.com.

Timothy Liu's books of poems are *For Dust Thou Art: Poems; Of Thee I Sing*, selected as a 2004 Book-of-the-Year by *Publishers Weekly; Hard Evidence; Say Goodnight; Burnt Offerings;* and *Vox Angelica* (winner of the 1992 Norma Farber First Book Award from the Poetry Society of America). His poetry has appeared in *Bomb, Field, Iowa Review, Kenyon Review, The Nation, New American Writing, Ploughshares, Paris Review, Poetry, Slate, Virginia Quarterly Review* and *The Yale Review*, among other publications. Reviews, articles, and essays of his have appeared in *Art Papers, New Art Examiner, Publishers Weekly*, and elsewhere. His poems have been translated into seven languages, and his journals and papers are archived in the Berg Collection at the New York Public Library. He has taught at the University of California, Berkeley; the University of Michigan; the University of North Carolina, Wilmington; and presently teaches at William Paterson University and in Bennington College's Writing Seminars. He lives in Manhattan.

Chip Livingston's poetry and fiction have appeared recently in Apalachee Review, Barrow Street, Cimarron Review, Mississippi Review, McSweeney's, and Ploughshares.

Raymond Luczak is the author and editor of eight books, including *Eyes of Desire 2: A Deaf GLBT Reader* and *Men with Their Hands*, first place winner of the Project: QueerLit 2006 Contest. His two books of poetry are *St. Michael's Fall* and *This Way to the Acorns*. His website is raymondluczak.com.

Ed Madden's first book of poetry, *Signals*, was selected by Afaa Weaver for the 2007 South Carolina Poetry Book prize and was published by the University of South Carolina Press in 2008. His poems have appeared in numerous journals, including *The Gay & Lesbian Review Worldwide*, *The James Dickey Newsletter*, *The Recorder: Journal of the American Irish Historical Society*, and *Los Angeles Review*, and in anthologies such as the Book of Irish American Poetry and the annual *Best New Poets 2007*. He is an associate professor of English and gender studies at the University of South Carolina.

Jeff Mann grew up in Covington, VA and Hinton, WV, receiving degrees in English and forestry from West Virginia University. His poetry, fiction, and essays have appeared in many publications, including *The Spoon River Poetry Review*, *Wild Sweet Notes: Fifty Years of West Virginia Poetry 1950-1999*, *Prairie Schooner*, *Shenandoah*, *Laurel Review*, *The Gay and Lesbian Review Worldwide*, *Crab Orchard Review*, *West Branch*, *Bloom*, and *Appalachian Heritage*. He has published three award-winning poetry chapbooks, *Bliss*, *Mountain Fireflies*, and *Flint Shards from Sussex*; two full-length books of poetry, *Bones Washed with Wine* and *On the Tongue*; a collection of personal essays, *Edge*; a book of poetry and memoir, *Loving Mountains, Loving Men*; and a volume of short fiction, *A History of Barbed Wire*, which won the Lambda Literary Award. He teaches creative writing at Virginia Tech in Blacksburg, Virginia.

Jaime Manrique was born in Colombia. His first book of poems received his country's National Book Award. He is the author of four novels: *Our Lives Are the Rivers, Twilight at the Equator, Latin Moon in Manhattan,* and *Colombian Gold,* the memoir *Eminent Maricones: Arenas, Lorca, Puig, and Me, as well as these* volumes of poems: M*y Night with Federico* García *Lorca*; *Tarzan, My Body, Christopher Columbus;* Sor *Juanaís Love Poems (*co-translated with Joan Larkin). His reviews have appeared in *The New York Times Book Review, Salon.com, Washington Post Book World, BOMB,* and many other publications. Among his honors are grants from the Foundation for Contemporary Performance Arts, and a John Simon Guggenheim Fellowship. In 2007, he received the International Latino Book Award (Historical Fiction). He is associate professor in the M.F.A. program in writing at Columbia University. Manrique is a Member of the Board of Trustees of PEN American Center.

Pablo Miguel Martínez's work has appeared in numerous publications, including Americas Review, Comstock Review, effing magazine, Gay & Lesbian Review, La Voz de Esperanza, San Antonio Current, and the San Antonio Express-News. In 2005 he was a recipient of the prestigious Chicano/Latino Literary Prize, and in 2003 he was awarded support from the Alfredo Cisneros Del Moral Foundation. Currently he teaches at Our Lady of the Lake University in San Antonio.

John McCullough's poetry has appeared in a range of publications including The Guardian, The Rialto, Smiths Knoll, Staple and Reactions and was the subject of a showcase feature in Magma in 2003. He teaches creative writing at the University of Sussex and the Open University and lives in Brighton. His most recent pamphlet is Cloudfish.

Billy Merrell is the author of *Talking in the Dark*, a poetry memoir, and a co-editor for *The Full Spectrum: A New Generation of Writing About LGBTQ and Other Identities*, which received a 2006 Lambda Literary Award. He received his M.F.A. in Poetry from Columbia University. Visit him online at billymerrell.com.

Jay Michaelson is the director of Nehirim: GLBT Jewish Culture and Spirituality (nehirim.org), the chief editor of Zeek: A Jewish Journal of Thought and Culture (zeek.net), and a columnist for the Forward newspaper. An active member of New York's "Pride in the Pulpit" project and a contributing editor of the White Crane Journal, Jay writes and teaches frequently on issues of sexuality and religion; his work has appeared on NPR, and in Tikkun, the Forward, Blithe House Quarterly, the Jerusalem Post, and anthologies including Charmed Lives, Mentsh and Righteous Indignation. Jay is a Ph.D candidate in Jewish Thought at Hebrew University, and also holds a J.D. from Yale. A recent finalist for the Koret Young Writer on Jewish Themes award, his most recent books are *God in Your Body* and *Another Word for Sky*. He can be found online at metatronics.net.

Miguel Murphy's first book of poetry *A Book Called Rats* won the Blue Lynx Prize, and he currently serves as Curating Editor for PISTOLA: a Journal of Poetry Online (pistolamag.org).

Billeh Nickerson is the author of *The Asthmatic Glassblower*, nominated for the Publishing Triangle Poetry Prize, and *Let Me Kiss it Better*. He is also co-editor of *Seminal: The Anthology of Canada's Gay Male Poets* with John

Barton; and a past editor of *Event* and *Prism international,* two of Canada's most respected literary journals. He lives in Vancouver, where he works as an event programmer for the Vancouver International Writers Festival and teaches creative writing at Kwantlen University College.

Christopher Nield's poetry has been published by *PN Review, The London Magazine, Ambit, The Rialto, The Keats-Shelley Review* and *Chroma* and features in *New Poetries IV.* In 2006 he was one of the winners of the Keats-Shelley prize.

Peter Pereira is a family physician at High Point Community Clinic in West Seattle. His poems have appeared in *Poetry, Prairie Schooner, New England Review, Journal of the American Medical Association,* and elsewhere. His books include *The Lost Twin, Saying the World (*winner of the Hayden Carruth Award and finalist for the Lambda Literary Award, the Publishing Triangle Award, and the PEN West Award), and *What's Written On the Body.* He lives in Seatttle with his partner, Dean Allan.

Carl Phillips is the author of numerous books of poetry, most recently *Quiver of Arrows: Selected Poems 1986-2006* and *Riding Westward.* His collection *The Rest of Love* won the Theodore Roethke Memorial Foundation Poetry Prize and the Thom Gunn Award for Gay Male Poetry, and was a finalist for the National Book Award. His other books include: *Rock Harbor; The Tether,* winner of a Kingsley Tufts Poetry Award; *Pastoral,* winner of a Lambda Literary Award; *From the Devotions,* finalist for the National Book Award; *Cortége,* finalist for the National Book Critics Circle Award; and *In the Blood,* winner of the Samuel French

Morse Poetry Prize. His honors include the 2006 Academy of American Poets Fellowship, an Award in Literature from the American Academy of Arts and Letters, the Pushcart Prize, the Academy of American Poets Prize, induction into the American Academy of Arts and Sciences, and fellowships from the Guggenheim Foundation and the Library of Congress. Phillips is Professor of English and of African and Afro-American Studies at Washington University in St. Louis, where he also teaches in the Creative Writing Program.

Kenneth Pobo's new book of poems, *Glass Garden*, released in 2008. His work appears in such journals as Indiana Review, Nimrod, Forpoetry.com, The Fiddlehead, and elsewhere. He teaches English and Creative Writing at Widener University in Pennsylvania.

Andy Quan is the author of two books of poetry, *Slant* and *Bowling Pin Fire*, as well as two collections of short fiction, *Calendar Boy* and *Six Positions*. He is also the co-editor of *Swallowing Clouds: An Anthology of Chinese Canadian Poetry*. Of Cantonese origin, he was born in Vancouver and has lived in Toronto, Brussels, and London, England. Also a singer and songwriter, he makes his home in Sydney, Australia, where he works on regional and international HIV and AIDS issues.

Steven Reigns is a Los Angeles based poet and educator. He earned a degree in Creative Writing at the University of South Florida, and taught writing workshops around the country to gay youth and people living with HIV. His published work includes the collection, *Your Dead Body is My Welcome Mat*, as well as two chapbooks, *Ignited* and *Cartography*. He served for three years as Literary

Director for Tampa's GLBT community center. Currently he is working on S(t)even Years, a 7-year endurance performance under the mentorship of performance artist Linda Montano and is also at work on a new collection of poetry titled *Inheritance*. He recently edited *My Life is Poetry*, an anthology of autobiographical poetry by GLB seniors. He can be found online at stevenreigns.com.

Shane Rhodes' first book, *The Wireless Room*, won the Alberta Book Award for poetry. His second book, *Holding Pattern*, won the Archibald Lampman Award. Shane is also featured in the anthologies *New Canadian Poetry, Breathing Fire II, Decalogue,* and *Seminal: Canada's Gay Male Poets.* His most recent book, *The Bindery*, released in 2007.

Jason Roush is the author of three books of poems: *After Hours, Breezeway,* and *Crosstown* (forthcoming from Windstorm Creative in 2009). His poetry and reviews have appeared in *Bay Windows, Brooklyn Review, Cimarron Review, The Gay & Lesbian Review Worldwide, Provincetown Magazine*, and elsewhere. He currently teaches writing, literature, and cultural studies at Emerson College in Boston and can be found online at jasonroush.com.

Jason Schneiderman is the author of *Sublimation Point*, a Stahlecker Selection from Four Way Books. He has received fellowships from Yaddo, The Fine Arts Work Center in Provincetown, and the Bread Loaf Writer's Conference. He received the 2004 Emily Dickinson Award from the Poetry Society of America. His poems have appeared in *American Poetry Review, The Best American Poetry (2005), Tin House, Poetry London,* and the *Penguin Book of the Sonnet*. He lives in Brooklyn with his husband Michael Broder.

Gregg Shapiro is a pop-culture journalist whose interviews and reviews run in a variety of regional LGBT publications and websites. His poetry and fiction have appeared in numerous outlets including literary journals such as Beltway, modern words, Bloom, White Crane Journal, Blithe House Quarterly, Mipoesias, and the anthologies *Sex & Chocolate: Tasty Morsels for Mind and Body*, *Queer Quarterly 2007* and *Blood to Remember*. His collection of poems, *Protection*, is forthcoming from Gival Press. He lives in Chicago with his life-partner Rick and their dogs, Dusty and k.d.

Reginald Shepherd was the author of five collections of poetry: *Fata Morgana; Otherhood* (a finalist for the Lenore Marhsall Poetry Prize); *Wrong; Angel, Interrupted;* and *Some Are Drowning* (winner of the Associated Writing Programs' Award in Poetry). He was the editor of *The Iowa Anthology of New American Poetries*, and his own work appeared in four editions of *The Best American Poetry*, as well as many other anthologies. He received grants from the National Endowment for the Arts, the Illinois Arts Council, and the Florida Arts Council, among many other awards and honors. He lived with his partner in Pensacola, Florida.

D. Antwan Stewart received his M.F.A. in Writing from the Michener Center for Writers, where he was a James A. Michener Fellow in poetry. His chapbooks, *The Terribly Beautiful* and *Sotto Voce* (forthcoming), were finalists in the Main Street Rag Poetry Chapbook Series. Other poems appear or will appear in *Meridian*, *Callaloo*, *The Seattle Review*, *Lodestar Quarterly*, *Bloom*, *storySouth*, *Poet Lore*, *New Millennium Writings*, and others.

Scott Wiggerman has published one book of poetry, *Vegetables and Other Relationships* and been published in dozens of journals, including *Gertrude, Windhover, Midwest Poetry Review, Spillway, Poesia,* and *modern words.* He was also included in the anthology *This New Breed: Gents, Bad Boys, and Barbarians 2.* In addition, he is one of the two "cats" (i.e., editors) of Dos Gatos Press, which publishes the *Texas Poetry Calendar,* now in its tenth year.

Gregory Woods is a poet, literary critic and teacher. His poetry collections are *We Have the Melon, May I Say Nothing, The District Commissioner's Dreams* and *Quidnunc,* all from Carcanet Press. His critical works include *Articulate Flesh: Male Homo-eroticism and Modern Poetry* and *A History of Gay Literature: The Male Tradition,* both from Yale University Press. He is professor of gay and lesbian studies at Nottingham Trent University, England.

Emanuel Xavier is the author of the poetry collections *Pier Queen* and *Americano,* the novel *Christlike,* and editor of *Bullets & Butterflies* and *Mariposas: A Modern Anthology of Queer Latino Poetry.* He has been featured on *Russell Simmons presents Def Poetry* on HBO. He performs regularly throughout the country as an openly gay spoken word artist and is considered a role model for queer youth, particularly queer youth of color. He is recipient of the Marsha A. Gomez Cultural Heritage Award and a NYC Council Citation for his many contributions to gay, Latino and New York City arts.

C. Dale Young is the author of two collections of poetry: *The Second Person* and *The Day Underneath the Day.* His third book of poetry, *TORN,* will be released by Four Way

Books in 2012. He practices medicine full-time, edits poetry for New England Review, and teaches in the Warren Wilson M.F.A. Program. He lives with his husband, the composer Jacob Bertrand, in San Francisco.

BIBLIOGRAPHY OF GAY–INTEREST POETRY TITLES FROM 2007

We have tried to be both accurate and comprehensive in the titles included as well as in the information about them. That said, there are certainly books that will have escaped our attention or which we were unable to obtain. Publishers, authors, and readers are invited to submit chapbooks, collections, and anthologies of interest to readers of gay poetry published in 2008 for inclusion in the roundup of *BEST GAY POETRY 2009* to: A Midsummer Night's Press, 16 West 36th Street, Second Floor, New York NY 10018 bestgaypoetry@gmail.com

Chapbooks:

Payday Loans
Jee Leong Koh
Poets Wear Prada Press, Hoboken, New Jersey
poetswearpradanj.home.att.net
Chapbook of 30 sonnets written in April, one for each day of National Poetry Month, about love, sex, work, etc.

Alarum
by Chip Livingston
Other Rooms Press, Brooklyn, New York
otherroomspress.blogspot.com
otherroomspress@gmail.com

22 page saddle stapled chapbook with 17 poems, in a wide range of styles and voices, many of them of interest to gay readers, such as "poem to my boyfriend's human immunodeficiency virus"

Books:

Blind Date With Cavafy
Steve Fellner
Marsh Hawk Press, P.O. Box 206
East Rockaway, NY 11518-0206
marshhawkpress.org
71 Pages, $12.50, ISBN 0-9785555-2-X
Winner of the Marsh Hawk Press Poetry Prize 2006 and the Thomas Gunn Award for Gay Male Poetry.

These fun, sometimes gonzo, poems, reminiscent of a gay Denise Duhamel (who was judge for the contest this book won), draw equally on classical and pop cultural icons and references, in a wild romp that sometimes seems a poetic equivalent of a good gossip and bitch session over brunch.

Torso
Robert Hamberger
Redbeck Press, 24 Aireville Road,
Frizinghall, Bradford, BD9 4HH UK
98 Pages, £7.95, ISBN 978-1-904338-25-3

This third collection by British poet Hamberger boasts many formal poems about subjects ranging from family life to the desire that burns between men, using both contemporary and classical allusions.

A Dream Of Adonis
David Brendan Hopes
Pecan Grove Press, Box AL, 1 Camino Santa Maria,
San Antonio, TX 78228
library.stmarytx.edu/pgpress
91 pages, $15, ISBN 978-1-951247-42-9

A collection of poems by a gay poet although much of the work is not explicitly gay, or only obliquely so: not a judgment of the poems so much as the content in the context of readers of this anthology.

Made Beautiful By Use
Sean Horlor
Signature Editions, Winnipeg, Manitoba (Canada)
signature-editions.com
69 pages, $12.95 US, ISBN 978-1-89710-913-7

This first collection by a promising young Canadian poet is full of exquisite poems that mix classical forms and references with urban, street-wise contemporary concerns such as homelessness, STDs and politics. Horlor works in a number of series, many of whose individual poems are perfect unto themselves, and take on even greater import or resonance in the context of his hagiographic and liturgical sequences.

Another Word For Sky
Jay Michaelson
Lethe Press, Maple Shade, NJ
lethepressbooks.com
103 pages, $14.95, ISBN 978-1-59021-061-1

A collection of poems that delve into both the mystical

and the physical aspects of gay life and relationships. Strong Jewish (and gay Jewish) and Buddhist content permeates this collection as well.

Banalities
Brane Mozetic
Translated by Elizabeth Zargi with Timothy Liu
A Midsummer Night's Press, New York, NY
www.amidsummernightspress.com
In these 50 poems translated from the Slovene, Mozetic confronts meaninglessness and pleasure, melancholy and excitement, often focusing on the pain we inflict on one another and especially the pain we inflict on ourselves. (Full disclosure: I published this book in English as editor of A Midsummer Night's Press.)

What's Written On The Body
Peter Pereira
Copper Canyon Press, Port Townsend, Washington
coppercanyonpress.org
103 pages, $15, ISBN 978-1-55659-252-2
   One of my favorite collections for the human warmth in these playful and touching poems wherein Pereira shares a domestic intimacy--with his lover, as a doctor--that left me with a dilemma (or trilemma) of which poems to select for this anthology.

Since I Moved In
Tim Peterson
Chax Press, Tucson, Arizona
chax.org
92 pages, $16, ISBN 978-0-925904-64-5
Winner of the Gil Ott Award.
   Of particular interest from this first collection is the

opening sequence, "Trans Figures," which both literally and figuratively embodies the poetic voice in search of itself and its expression, in language and form.

Bowling Pin Fire
Andy Quan
Signature Editions, Winnipeg, Manitoba (Canada)
signature-editions.com
71 pages, $12.95 US, ISBN 978-1-89710-922-9

Quan's second collection of poems dances between exploration of new experiences and the impact of memories—of lost loves, of childhood—as both the poet and his concerns move along the arc of life out of the first headlong flush of youth into a more seasoned (and contemplative) maturity.

The Bindery
Shane Rhodes
Newest Press, Edmonton, Alberta (Canada)
100 pages, $12.95 US, ISBN 978-1-897126-14-1

Rhodes' latest book explores dispersion and cohesion in a fragmentary (quite literally in the case of the title poem) collection that uses ekphrastic poems and travel as the backdrop upon which he pushes language and syntax to unsettle the conventional lyric.

Breezeway
Jason Roush
Windstorm Creative,
Port Orchard, Washington
windstormcreative.com
76 Pages, $9.99, ISBN 978-1-59092-371-9

A collection of lyrical poems that often find meaning in small moments, crafted with a precision of language and syntax that is nonetheless accessible and immediate.

Fata Morgana
Reginald Shepherd
University of Pittsburgh Press
upress.pitt.edu
104 pages, $14 ISBN 978-0-82295-951-9

Shepherd's fifth collection is at the same time a meditation on loss and a celebration of "song," steeped in mythology and personal history both. He often writes about that which is just out of our grasp, whether physical or spiritual, elusive as the chimera (*fata morgana*) of the title, and how it is the yearning for and striving for that creates beauty and meaning.

Anthologies:

Seminal: The Anthology Of Canada's Gay Male Poets
edited by John Barton and Billeh Nickerson
Arsenal Pulp Press, Vancouver, Canada
arsenalpulp.com
368 pages, $21.95 US, ISBN 978-1-55152-217-3

A groundbreaking anthology of Canadian gay male poetry, historical in its scope, covering work from 1890 to the present, with an important introduction to give the context of gay poetry within Canada's poetry world and the larger English-speaking poetry scene.

Voices Rising: Celebrating 20 Years Of Black Lesbian, Gay, Bisexual And Transgender Writing
edited by G. Winston James and Other Voices
RedBone Press, PO Box 15571 Washington, DC 20003
redbonepress.com
583 Pages, $25, ISBN 978-0-9786251-3-9

This comprehensive anthology, published to mark the

twentieth anniversary of Other Countries, an organization devoted to black queer expression, is an important document of the struggles and achievements of black gays, lesbians, bisexuals, and transgendered people as expressed in a mix of essays, stories, and poems by over 60 contributors.

The Wind Shifts: New Latino Poetry
edited by Francisco Aragón
University of Arizona Press
uapress.arizona.edu
266 pages, ISBN 978-0-8165-2493-8

While not a gay anthology, this collection of new latino voices includes relevant work by Steven Cordova (including one poem reprinted herein), and interesting work by Eduardo C. Corral and the editor, Francisco Aragón

Grateful acknowledgment is made for permission to reprint the following material:

"In Front of Everyone" © 2007 by Antler. First published in *Knockout* (online). Reprinted by permission of the author.

"Slow Change" © 2007 by Rane Arroyo. First published in *Bryant Literary Review* 8 (2007): 114. Reprinted by permission of the author.

"Fences" © 2007 by John Barton. First published as a Poem of the Week on the website of the Parliamentary Poet Laureate (Canada), December 10-16, 2007. Reprinted by permission of the author.

"The Crossing" © 2007 Dan Bellm. "The crossing" was written for the Shabbat evening prayer book of Congregation Sha'ar Zahav, the LGBT synagogue of San Francisco; it first appeared in *Prairie Schooner*, Spring 2007, in a special section called "Yidishkayt: Poetry and Prose." Reprinted by permission of the author.

"The Embrace" © 2007 David Bergman. First published in *Bloom*. Reprinted by permission of the author.

"The Estate Auction" © 2007 James Cihlar. First published in the anthology *Nebraska Presence* (Backwaters Press, 2007). Reprinted by permission of the author.

"The Play" © 2007 by Jeffery Conway. First published in *Milk*, Summer 2007. Reprinted by permission of the author.

"Across a Table" © 2003 by Steven Cordova. First published in *Slow Dissolve* by Steven Cordova (momotombo Press, 2003). Reprinted from *The Wind Shifts: New Latino Poetry* (University of Arizona Press, 2007) by permission of the author.

"Hybrid" © 2007 by James Crandall. First published in Issue #23 of the on-line journal *In Posse Review*. Reprinted by permission of the author.

"How to Write a Love Poem" © 2007 by James Crews. First published in *Forward*. Reprinted by permission of the author.

"Barebacking" © 2007 by Brian Cronwall. Frist published in *Chroma* Issue 6 (Spring 2007). Reprinted by permission of the author.

"I Am Known As Walt Whitman" © 2007 by Steve Fellner. First published in *TriQuarterly*. Reprinted by permission of the author.

"Once" © 2002 by John Frazier. Reprinted from *Voices Rising: Celebrating 20 Years of Black Lesbian, Gay, Bisexual & Transgender Writing*, edited by G. Winston James and Other Countries (RedBone Press, 2007) by permission of the author.

"Moon River" © 2007 by Brad Gooch. First published in *Bloom*. Reprinted by permission of the author.

"My City" © 2007 by Jeremy Halinen. First published in *Dos Passos Review*. Reprinted by permission of the author.

About the Editor

Lawrence Schimel is a full-time author and anthologist, who's published over 90 books, including *Two Boys in Love* (Seventh Window), *The Future is Queer* (Arsenal Pulp), *Best Date Ever: True Stories That Celebrate Gay Relationships* (Alyson), *The Drag Queen of Elfland* (Cleis), *His Tongue* (North Atlantic), *Kosher Meat* (Sherman Asher), *The Mammoth Book of New Gay Erotica* (Carroll & Graf), *Switch Hitters: Lesbians Write Gay Male Erotica and Gay Men Write Lesbian Erotica* (with Carol Queen; Cleis) and *Vacation in Ibiza* (NBM), among others. He has won the Lambda Literary Award twice, for *First Person Queer* (with Richard Labonte; Arsenal Pulp) and *PoMoSexuals: Challenging Assumptions About Gender and Sexuality* (with Carol Queen; Cleis), among other honors and awards. His first book of poems written in Spanish, *Desayuno en la cama* (Desatada/Egales) was published in 2008. He won the Rhysling Award for Poetry in 2002. His work has been widely anthologized in *The Random House Book of Science Fiction Stories, The Best of Best Gay Erotica, Gay Love Poetry, The Mammoth Book of Gay Short Stories, The Mammoth Book of Comic Fantasy, The Mammoth Book of Fairy Tales,*

Chicken Soup for the Horse-Lover's Soul 2, and *The Random House Treasury of Light Verse,* among many others. He has also contributed to numerous periodicals, from *The Christian Science Monitor* to *Physics Today* to *Gay Times.* His writings have been translated into Basque, Catalan, Croatian, Czech, Dutch, Esperanto, Finnish, French, Galician, German, Greek, Hungarian, Indonesian, Italian, Japanese, Polish, Portuguese, Romanian, Russian, Slovak, and Spanish. For two years he served as co-chair of the Publishing Triangle, a US organization of lesbians and gay men in the publishing industry, and he also served as the Regional Advisor of the Spain Chapter of the Society of Children's Book Writers and Illustrators for five years. Born in New York City in 1971, he lives in Madrid, Spain.

Printed in the United States
146118LV00001B/43/P